Meditation

Meditation

SAHAJ MARG

EDUCATIONAL SERIES

Volume 1

Compiled by Ferdinand Wulliemier

Sahaj Marg Research Institute

SHRI RAM CHANDRA MISSION

Shri Ram Chandra Mission
Post Office Box 269
Molena, GA 30258
U.S.A.

http://www.srcm.org/srcm/

First Edition: February, 1997

Printed in United States of America

04 03 02 01 00 99 98 97 8 7 6 5 4 3 2 1

ISBN 0-945242-34-4

Contents

Preface

The compilation of this series of texts on Sahaj Marg literature, beginning with the present theme of meditation, was suggested officially by our living Master, Shri Parthasarathi Rajagopalachari, during the speech he delivered to the participants of the Sahaj Marg Research Institute (SMRI) seminar in Pratharham, 26 November 1992.

The following quotations from this talk have guided us:

"I have a few suggestions to make. One is that the Sahaj Marg Research Institute should try to compile textbooks on Sahaj Marg. It should be limited to extracting what Babuji has said about meditation in all his writings, for example, as volume one: 'Meditation by Ram Chandra', you see. Lalaji's quotations of course can also be added, as being the Adi-Guru of the system. Similarly, there might be a second volume on constant remembrance; there could be a third volume on cleaning; there can be a fourth volume on ethics and moral considerations under the Sahaj Marg system. So if you have a set of three or four books like that, comprising the Sahaj Marg textbooks series, authentic teachings of Lalaji and Babuji Maharaj, I think that would be a very good foundation for the training of our abhyasis and, perhaps more importantly, of our preceptors. ...

"The body of literature originating from Babuji's and Lalaji's hands is not to be thought of as textbooks. They are great books, they are holy books, but not textbooks. Textbooks teach. ...

"It is necessary to recast that same literature into different specific moulds, subjectwise, so my first request to the SMRI, to its director and its faculty is to get on with this job of compilation, exactly as said by Babuji Maharaj. No deviation, no translation – first in English. I say this because when I was participating in the seminar on prayer the other day—teaching course on prayer—I found so many opinions were expressed. ...

"Now that should be the real job of the SMRI and it should do this job very quickly, because it is essential that abhyasis should know what is Sahaj Marg. ...

"If you don't understand Sahaj Marg properly, you will not practise Sahaj Marg properly."

In January 1993 an informal conversation took place in Manapakkam with Chariji, which brought in the following additions and clarifications:

- The writings of Shri P. Rajagopalachari will also be taken into consideration for these textbooks. I had to insist on this point, Chariji arguing that he had only repeated, sometimes in another way, what his Master had said.
- The Sahaj Marg literature to be classified into four main headings:
    1. *The Sahaj Marg process*—including meditation, cleaning, constant remembrance, prayer, and the ten maxims.
    2. *The goal of Sahaj Marg*—including liberation, realisation, human perfection, and mergence.
    3. *Subsidiaries*—including faith, devotion, love, co-operation, will, surrender, etc.
    4. *Impediments*—which are of course more numerous because they have to deal with our grossness, including samskaras, desires, emotions, egotism, fanaticism, doubts, excitation, greed, guilt, etc.

The first draft of the present book was brought to Chariji for Basant 1995, showing that, despite his recommendation, we were not particularly quick in this job, at least at the outset when only three abhyasis were working on it.

This first edition contains excerpts from a total of thirty-eight books, published up to and including *Revealing the Personality*, released in 1994. Only two books published during this time, *In His Footsteps*, Volume II, and *Proceedings of the Preceptor's Seminar*, did not contain any significant quotations on meditation.

According to the *neti-neti* (not this-not this) tradition, we have included a short section entitled 'What Meditation Is Not', in order to clarify our understanding of this fundamental subject. We did not try for an exhaustive compilation since our primary purpose was to discriminate between meditation, concentration, and hypnotism.

The excerpts are presented chronologically as far as possible. The exceptions are when we have respected the continuity of series like *The Principles of Sahaj Marg* or *Heart to Heart*. Some books already published are not included because they were already the result of compilations of previously published talks or quotations. This is the case for *Face to Face*, *Evolution Towards Divinity*, and, of course, *Deva Vani*, which may be considered as the ancestor of the present series. As far as *India in the West*, *Sahaj Marg in Europe*, and *Blossoms in the East* are concerned, we printed under those titles only what was not already printed in *Principles of Sahaj Marg,* volumes I and II, in order to avoid unnecessary repetition. A reference list of the specific editions used appears at the end of the book.

In the selected passages some sentences were disregarded which only mentioned the word 'meditation' without any further explanation on the topic. On the other hand, several rather similar passages were kept in toto because there were some useful or helpful differences in the description or explanations about this crucial part of our meditation method. Only once has a passage been repeated twice, as it appears in the original writings of Babuji himself (pages 135 and 340 of *Complete Works of Ram Chandra*, Volume I).

Some passages describing two terms, like meditation and concentration, have not been artificially divided into the two parts of this book. They may appear in both 'What Meditation Is Not', and 'What Meditation Is'.

We tried as far as possible to avoid the loss of relevant information. Nevertheless, this being a human work, and our method of indexing keywords having been refined and expanded during the three years of pilot work, some mistakes may have been made despite our good will and intentions. In that case, we would be thankful to our brothers and sisters to make us aware of these imperfections so that we can make the necessary corrections for a second edition.

There is no doubt these compilations will be very useful to the abhyasis willing to go deeper into the numerous subjects proposed for the complete series. This will certainly also help us to acquire the necessary broad view of each subject. Reading these books repeatedly may also prevent the tendency to divide what we read into the parts we feel comfortable with, and ignoring or forgetting the parts which don't please us.

Last, but not least, let us repeat the wish expressed by Chariji in his Pratharham speech, namely that it will also help us, and especially abhyasis who teach others, to avoid opinion-minded talks, that is to say deviations issued from our own fantasies which our ego is so prone to produce.

Ferdinand Wulliemier

Acknowledgements

We are very thankful to our living Master, Shri P. Rajagopalachari, to have inspired us and permitted us to realise the product of this teamwork, which we hope will become more and more trans-national in the future when the other volumes of this series will be produced. This present text on meditation would not have been published without the help of the following dedicated workers:

Margot Asso
Kanyhama Dixon-Fyle
Patrick Eldaray
Alfred Hüppmeir
Simone Hubert
Henri Mercier
Vincent Piguet
François Poirier
Anne-Marie Potin
Christine Prisland
Christine Rappaz
Jean-Phil Rebeyrotte
Nicole Renevey
Gabrielle Schoeb
Claudine Sidwell
Charles Treichler
Martine Van Overloop
Diana Waycott
Nicole Wickihalder
Catherine Wulliemier

Lalaji
Shri Ram Chandraji of Fatehgarh, U.P.
Adi-Guru, Shri Ram Chandra Mission

Babuji
Shri Ram Chandraji of Shahjahanpur, U.P.
Founder-President, Shri Ram Chandra Mission

Chariji
Shri Partharsarathi Rajagopalachariji
President, Shri Ram Chandra Mission

"If you don't understand Sahaj Marg properly,

you will not practise Sahaj Marg properly"

Shri P. Rajagopalachari

Part One

What Meditation Is Not

Cleaning

A Preceptor's Guide, Volume II
Shri P. Rajagopalachari

I think in Courmettes I had a discussion about meditation and cleaning, what is the basic difference. The basic difference is that in meditation your mind is brought to a state of passivity applied to a single object to promote or develop concentration, and there it rests. There is no question of will power during meditation. In cleaning there is no meditation, there is only the application of will power used to remove grossness, impurities, complexes... (p.125)

CONCENTRATION

Complete Works of Ram Chandra, Volume I
Shri Ram Chandra

Concentration is the automatic and natural result of meditation. Those who insist on concentration in place of meditation, and force their mind to it, generally meet with failure. (p.342)

Complete Works of Ram Chandra, Volume II
Shri Ram Chandra

Concentration, as commonly understood, refers to a state in which the conscious activity of the mind is brought to a standstill. But that is not the correct expression of the sense implied in it. This type of concentration implies physical effort which one must resort to consciously or even unconsciously. Usually, one proceeds with a conscious idea of some particular state which he interprets as concentration. Generally people take it in the sense of an unnatural heavy sleep brought about by the temporary suspension of the senses. As such, it is just like a state of senselessness caused by the drowning effect of some intoxicating drug. It may perhaps be for that very reason that some of the so-called mahatmas are found to be addicted to bhang, charas or ganja.

Generally, teachers advise the abhyasi to practise concentration as a preliminary step, and the abhyasi puts himself to efforts for effecting the same. But in spite of all his labour for years together he is seldom able to achieve it. Why is it so? The failure can in no way be attributed to any of the defects of the abhyasi but to that of the teacher himself, who resorts to his bookish knowledge to guide the aspirant on the practical path of Realisation. The fact is that the entire process, as it is prescribed, is wholly unnatural and artificial, and the means adopted for the purpose are all physical and gross. The result is that instead of proceeding towards subtleness, they go on imbibing more and more of solidity and grossness, and finally turn into impregnable rock.

Taking up concentration in terms of suspension of mental activities, one has necessarily to apply his effort to create in himself a state of insensibility. The force required for the purpose is undoubtedly the physical force which acts in combination with matter. Thus the whole process undertaken for the purpose becomes a material pursuit in the real sense. Concentration in that sense relates to the condition of the physical mind at the conscious level, the activity of which is temporarily subdued by the application of physical force. Practical examples offer sufficient proof to show that those having advanced with the condition thus developed, become wholly insusceptible to finer and subtler influences. Concentration effected by forceful suppression of thoughts leaves its weighty effect upon the mind. The force applied for the purpose, also being a physical force, causes its own weight. Thus in a word the state of concentration interpreted as coma is basically wrong, since it keeps one in close touch with matter. In that sense concentration may aptly be compared to a marshy condition, from which it is very difficult for one to extricate himself. He cannot save himself from sinking down deep into it unless he falls flat over it, giving up all his efforts. Those who proceed on with that condition, carry along all through with matter. It may however help them to some extent in their material purposes and promote in them hypnotic powers, but it is not the least helpful in a purely spiritual pursuit.

People like to go into concentration because it is pleasing to the senses. Obviously it cannot, therefore, be helpful in a spiritual pursuit. Concentration directly refers to suppression of thoughts. The idea entered into our mind only after mesmerism or hypnotism had come to our view, because there the physical force of thought was utilised all through. No spiritual purpose can be served thereby. It can, however, reveal the nature and character of a thing, but that can by no means help its achievement. It cannot therefore be instrumental in the attainment of God. On the other hand it tends to keep away from Reality. The basis of meditation is purely spiritual, while that of concentration is only the ego. When you mean to concentrate, 'you' are there, quite definitely, but when you meditate, you wait for something higher, hence you are away from the idea of self.

The only proper course for an aspirant would therefore be to get himself absorbed in the light of the Divine coming to him from the Original source, without minding the implications of the word concentration. In that case the question of concentration will not arise at all, and one will all along be with that which can neither be interpreted as concentration nor otherwise. Concentration with all its implications affecting enclosement, being not of any avail, it is only the power of 'non-concentration' as I may call it that enables one's approach to higher and higher regions of enlightenment. Proceeding along in that way, one would keep on imbibing the power of the Source to light himself up with Divine effulgence.

Now what condition does the word 'non-concentration' refer to? Obviously it refers to a state associated with an overflow of thoughts. But then there are two aspects of it: the one when the flow is not conjoined with our conscious knowledge, and the other when we have a conscious awareness of it, and take its effect upon the mind. This, the latter one, may no doubt amount to a state of distraction, especially when one is linked with the thought of some misery or affliction. In the former case, though the flow continues uninterruptedly, yet the encumbering effect thereof is not felt upon the mind. Normally this state of mind is seldom found to be disturbing. Taking these two aspects into view I might say that the latter is quite similar to the state known as concentration, but with only this difference that here the object of concentration is one's distraction and worry instead of the Godly thought. It may therefore be taken as crude concentration which is maintained by the force of our unconscious efforts. The effect in both the cases (viz., by conscious effort and by unconscious effort) is the same, i.e., heaviness, dullness, sluggishness. The very word concentration implies a sense of artificiality, and effort is for that reason indispensable. When the flow of thought is spontaneous it is effortless and closely similar to the state commonly known as concentration. The proper word for that may therefore be 'absorption', which is a natural course and follows by itself as the result of meditation on the right lines.

Concentration taken in the sense of absorption (non-concentration, with flow of thoughts, without effect on the mind) is the real state. It may be of different types at different levels. One may be the concentration of the lower level, another that of the higher level, and still another that of the highest level. Now taking out the common factor 'concentration' from these, what remains thereafter is only the lower, the higher and the highest. That is how one has to go on with his march towards the Ultimate. On the other hand if our thought remains involved with the idea of concentration, the inner force will not be working actively to offer us impetus for our higher ascent. The proper course would therefore be to take up the thought in the form of *sankalpa* (subtle idea) without any imposed resolve or effort, and proceed on with it in a gentle and natural way without enforcing any artificiality or imposition. Such is the process followed in Sahaj Marg which, as a matter of fact, introduces through the Master's *pranahuti* from the very beginning that very state which lies at the farthest end. Though in the beginning one might have, at times, only glimpses of it, yet after continued practice the same condition covers him all over. This is why in spite of the continuity of thoughts often present at the time of meditation, one proceeding by Sahaj Marg experiences a peculiar state of concentration better interpreted as 'absorption'. (p.72-77)

Autobiography of Ram Chandra, Volume I
Shri Ram Chandra

Concentration is one of the instruments for revelation only. You cannot 'get' God by concentration. In concentration you are one-pointed to a certain object, while in meditation your subconscious only waits for something. (p.9)

— ❖ —

Concentration is the Divine instrument for revelation. People are of the opinion that if there is no concentration, meditation is useless. I can emphatically say that a man can never 'get' God by concentration, because in concentration you are one-pointed and you are not waiting for anything, while in meditation you wait for something and that is God. (p.30)

Messages Universal
Shri Ram Chandra

While referring to this path to the Ultimate, saints have said, "beyond and beyond." When we speak thus, it sounds very well. But when we try to do it, things become a bit difficult, for due preparation is not there. 'I' consciousness remains far and near, and it disappears also, if we do our *abhyas* devotedly. There is a common error almost everywhere, that they think 'I' as an enemy. That is a negative attachment, which makes it hard and impossible. When we think of 'I', it becomes stronger by our own thought force, brought about by concentration. Try to forget the 'I', it will help a good deal. Once Divinity dawns, the negative attitude to life goes far away. The demolition of the past is a chapter in Sahaj Marg. (p.179)

My Master
Shri P. Rajagopalachari

"You can 'read' the atmosphere of a place and see what sort of events have taken place there. It is very easy. Just concentrate, and the reading will appear before your eyes. If you go beyond this you can even concentrate on the atmosphere in a general way and 'read' a country's history in it. What happened, when, everything is there. The records of everything are there, clear as anything, but it needs only one who can 'see' to read all this." [Babuji] (p.18)

— ❖ —

"This is the reason why we start with the heart in our *sanstha*. If the heart is purified then that purity extends throughout the system. The circulation is controlled by the heart. Really speaking this is where the process must really commence. Other points are there as have been taken up by other systems, such as the point of the nose, the point between the eyebrows and so on. But we start with the heart. We take up the heart for our work. Other points for concentration may be good for *siddhis*, for acquiring powers and for limited growth." [Babuji] (p.113)

— ❖ —

"Now people talk of concentration. Concentration is the method of revelation. Meditation is the method of realisation. Concentration can reveal the nature of the object or thing concentrated upon, but it cannot lead to realisation. If you want to know the condition of an abhyasi just concentrate upon it, and the condition will come before you. Verify with the heart and it will give you the signal whether it is correct. But I am telling you a very important thing. Concentration can reveal everything but not God. If you concentrate upon God you cannot see Him because there is no thought! Only the Divine can see the Divine!" [Babuji] (p.159-160)

Principles of Sahaj Marg, Volume V
Shri P. Rajagopalachari

Concentration is nothing but a stage in which the mind can rest on a particular object at my choice, at my will, for as long as I choose. That is concentration. Concentration is not an act, it is a state of mind, a state of existence. Then the mind, which has now become capable of concentration under my command, is my instrument. (p.70)

Principles of Sahaj Marg, Volume VIII
Shri P. Rajagopalachari

Very often, when I sit in these meetings, Sahaj Marg meetings, and people are talking, I go into meditation and I cannot keep my eyes open. And then some girl comes and says, "Oh Chari! You are very sleepy." I get a bad name. But I am not sleepy. Because with one part of me, I am trying to concentrate. The concentration makes me go into meditation. Same thing happens to music. I used to go to lot of music performances. I stopped fifteen years ago. Because I go with my wife and I am sitting in the music hall, full, and the moment I start listening to the music, you know, and my wife says, "Wake up, people know me, what will they think?" But I am not sleeping. So I asked Master. He said, "You know when you meditate properly, you reach a stage of concentration; now, when you concentrate you go into meditation"—the reverse. That is why we are not able to read books any more, you see. Because when you read with concentration, the mind goes inside and the book is gone and people think you are sleeping. But it is not sleep, you follow? So the reversibility, you see. (p.200)

Heart to Heart, Volume III
Shri P. Rajagopalachari

We try to bring the mind to regulation by keeping it on one object all the time. And through that, achieve a state of concentration which, incidentally, is another error in most English translations of yoga books, that very often meditation is treated as a technique for concentration. Very simply, meditation means to think continuously about one thing. and by repeated practice, when we are able to achieve that condition, we have developed the ability to concentrate. And then, anything on which you put your mind, it is revealed to you.

So the mind becomes an instrument of revelation, and therefore it is said such rishis could see into the future and see into the past. But here again my Master gave me a warning, "God is not an object. He is not a physical being. He has no position anywhere specifically in the universe. Therefore, He cannot be an object of concentration. Therefore, however powerful the mind may be, whatever fantastic powers of concentration you may develop, the Divine can never be revealed by that." (p.106-107)

— ❖ —

Unfortunately, many people say many things about meditation. And I think the Sanskrit literature itself has to take a substantial degree of blame for it, where instead of talking of meditation, it talks more of concentration. And we hear this cry from human being after human being, "How can I concentrate? My mind is not mine you see. I cannot think of something for two minutes and you are asking me to concentrate." Now, my Master explained this very beautifully. He said, "Meditation is to think continuously of something. It is a process. You have to make the effort and progressively, as you are able to hold your mind on that thought for longer and longer periods of time, you come to a state where the mind is totally on that, you see, and that is concentration."

So concentration is the result of a process. Concentration is a state of mind, Unfortunately most people, I think almost all people, talk of concentration as if they are, you know, creating coffee in a coffee machine, using the physical analogy of creating a concentrated solution, boiling off the water. (p.163-164)

In His Footsteps, Volume I
Shri P. Rajagopalachari

D: But should we not try to concentrate?
Dr. KCV[Dr. K.C. Varadachari]: Concentrate on what? If you mean some work like an accounting calculation or something like that, then certainly you ought to concentrate. You can concentrate on small things like that. But can you concentrate on the sky? Can you pin-point your mind on the sky? You see what I mean? If you try to 'concentrate' on the sky, you only see a star, or a bird, or a small cloud, or some such thing. You don't see the sky. That is why in this system we don't do it. I mean concentration, or pin-pointing the mind as you call it. We don't do it, firstly because it is very difficult, and secondly it is a strain. Concentration, or the attempt to concentrate produces tremendous strain. Concentration needs attention.

What we should do is not to attend, but to 'detend' to remove the tension, to relax. Have you ever noticed some people who really admire natural scenery? They don't concentrate on the scene. They relax and sit down or lie down, and absorb nature into them. They don't 'see' anything, but they are absorbing everything simultaneously, and therefore really seeing everything all at once—not bit by disjointed bit. That is the only way in which one can see the sky, or a scene, or anything big. As I said, we should not attend or concentrate, but 'detend', relax. How can you then pin-point the Divine, the Ultimate? No!

D: But should we not try to concentrate on the Divine?

Dr. KCV: Can you do it? That is the whole problem. Can you pin-point the omni-pervasive?

D: If He is omni-present, it should be possible, I think.

Dr. KCV: Now, be careful. I said omni-pervasive. He is omni-pervasive. He can be present if you need Him. That is precisely the point.

Now look at it this way. What are we? We are only points. After all, what is man in relation to the cosmos or the universe? He is just a point. Now you are a pin-point yourself. And you want to pin-point the Divine. You are an atom, and want to become a sub-atom. That is the problem.

Now, as Max Bohm has said, man, in relation to the atom on one side, and the cosmos on the other, stands almost midway between the two. If you try to concentrate, you are going towards the atom. You are restricting yourself. You are building up tensions. What is the result? You get the so-called yogis like Sankaracharya and Chinmayananda. (...) I ask you, what do you want? If you want achievements on the worldly plane, siddhis, etc., then the method of concentration maybe useful...

As I told you, Max Bohm has said that man is almost exactly between the atom and the universe. Now man is a pin-point himself. Isn't it? The mind of man is like a lens, which concentrates the universe or the cosmos into a pin-point, and that pin-point is man himself. I am therefore the point of my own mind, concentrated by my mind. So I am the product of my own concentration of my mind! You see that?

So what is needed is not concentration. It is a diffusion, or a dispersion that is really needed. The concentrated point must be reversed and diffused back to its original source. Therefore concentration is not only unnecessary, it is not possible. (p.150-152)

Master [Babuji]: Concentration is the method for Revelation. Meditation is the method for Realisation. Concentration can reveal the nature of the object concentrated upon, but cannot lead to Realisation. (p.285)

HYPNOTISM

Complete Works of Ram Chandra, Volume II
Shri Ram Chandra

A crude analogy of this process [transmission] may be found in mesmerism and hypnotism whose results are contrary to those of *pranahuti*. In these baser arts the hypnotizer uses his will-force with the backing of material power. And the will of the hypnotized person is weakened, and he finds himself dull and heavy-hearted after he wakes up from the hypnotic trance. A disease may be suppressed to some extent, depending upon the power of the hypnotizer and the submission of the hypnotized. But the effect does not last long. The hypnotic power is developed by some intense mental and physical practices using material things or mental images as objects of concentration. These practices often lead one to mental deformity or insanity, and sometimes even physical deformities will be the result. A successful practice, after a long time, may however result at the most in the gain of some material power which is limited, and useful only for the gratification of some kinds of desires as long as it lasts. (p.292)

WORSHIP

Principles of Sahaj Marg, Volume VIII
Shri P. Rajagopalachari

In this book which has recently been released, you will find there is a quotation from St. Augustine who says: If I worship stone, one who worships stone—becomes like stone; one who worships something else becomes like that. One who worships God, what will he become? "I dare not speak further, you may stone me." One who worships God must become like God, you see. We don't worship God to become millionaires. It is a lie. It is, shall we say, a breach of faith with the Almighty. So, as we worship, so we become; as we meditate, so we become. Why this distinction? Because in worship, at least in India, in the *sanatana dharma*, the Hindu hold, the worship is always associated with an external object of worship. Be it an idol, a picture, a form. Now, meditation removes this aspect of, shall we say, intercommunication with Divinity into a higher realm—the realm of thought. Raja yoga means precisely that—using the mind and its powers to achieve what we have to achieve. Now it seems to be a contradiction in terms that we use the mind but stick to a *sthool rupa* (gross form), or a *moorthy* (idol), or a mantra. So, this point my Master always wished to emphasize, that, "When we think of God, it should be in the abstract." God has no form. At least, when we think of Rama and Krishna, yes, but when we think of the Ultimate, the Paratatva, as we call it in our *dharma* (religion), the Paratatva has no *gunas* (attributes). It has no form, it has no attributes, it has no name. (p.147)

Part Two

What Meditation Is

Truth Eternal
Shri Ram Chandraji of Fatehgarh U.P.

(1) Remembrance, (2) Meditation, (3) Bhajan. When the practice of these three is associated with external things, the result would be birth and bondage. And when they are practised at heart internally keeping the goal constantly in view, it will result in freedom from external and surface bondage.

(1) Remembrance means remembering again and again,

(2) Meditation means having the idea,

(3) Bhajan means contemplation or continuous meditation.

(p.116)

Complete Works of Ram Chandra, Volume I
Shri Ram Chandra

The mind is like the pendulum of a clock. The clock goes all right so long as the movement of the pendulum is regulated. If it is disturbed the clock is out of order. Similarly for this human clock it is necessary that the movement of the mind be well regulated and adjusted. The methods to mould the mind and regulate its activities are also very simple. Really we have spoiled the mind ourselves by allowing it to wander about aimlessly during leisure hours. The practice has continued for years and it has now become almost its second nature. If we now try to control the mind by putting it under restraint we meet with little success. The more we try to suppress it by force, the more it rebounds and counteracts causing greater disturbance.

The proper method to control the activities of the mind is to fix it on one sacred thought just as we do in meditation, and dispel from it everything unwanted or superfluous. In course of time after constant practice, the mind gets disciplined and regulated and much of the inner disturbance is eliminated. The best course to free yourself from unwanted ideas is to treat them as uninvited guests and remain unmindful of them. They will then wither away like unwatered plants and ultimately the same sacred thought will remain predominant. The only way to accomplish it is, therefore, meditation under the guidance of a capable master. By constant practice in meditation the mind will become calm and peaceful and the unwanted ideas will cease to trouble you.

I often hear beginners complaining about the wandering of the mind during meditation. From the very first day they expect that during their practice at meditation the mind should remain at a standstill but when they find different ideas and thoughts haunting their mind they feel greatly perturbed. I must clear it to them that it is not the suspended condition of the mind we are striving for in our practice, but only the moulding of its multifarious activities. We do not want to stop its normal working but only to bring it to a regulated and disciplined state. If the activities of the mind are stopped from the very beginning, we probably do not stand in need of practising meditation at all. Meditation is the only process to achieve that end. Concentration is its natural result in due course. The proper method is to meditate all along remaining quite unmindful of the foreign ideas and thoughts coming to our mind during that time. (p.35-36)

— ❖ —

A most common excuse advanced by certain people today is that they are too busy to devote any time to meditation or similar other practice. But "the busiest man has the greatest leisure" is a well-known saying. I think a man has more time at his disposal than there is work for him to do. Their complaint of the scarcity of time is due only to its wrong adjustment. If we utilize our time to the best advantage we shall never have cause to complain that it is short or scarce. There are others who are a bit frank to admit that it is not for want of time that they remain away from devotional duties but for their habitual negligence and sluggishness which they cannot overcome. To them I would say that they are probably never negligent or sluggish in their trade or profession which they attend to with full zeal in spite of all personal inconvenience and even illness, only because some monetary gain or profit is in view. (p.37-38)

— ❖ —

Generally people complain of numerous ideas creeping into their mind at the time of meditation. They think that they have failed in their practice unless they bring their mind to a standstill. But it is not so. We are not practising concentration but only meditation. We must go on with meditation unmindful of the foreign ideas that happen to come to our mind at the time. The flow of ideas is due to the activities of our conscious mind which is never at rest. We are still busy in meditation with our subconscious mind, while our conscious mind is roaming about and forming numerous ideas. Thus we are not the loser in any way. In due course, after sufficient practice, the conscious mind too gets moulded and begins to act in harmony with the subconscious mind. The result thus achieved is deep-rooted and lasting, and finally calmness, the characteristic of soul, becomes predominant.

In certain cases I have observed the teachers exercising their will power to stop the normal functioning of the mind during sittings, creating a temporary state of senselessness or suspension of brain. The condition, no doubt, is most attractive to a beginner, who is ignorant of reality, and he feels greatly impressed by this extraordinary display of power. In my opinion it is only a feat of jugglery practised by those who are eager to attract the largest number of disciples in order to establish their greatness as a Guru. (p.69-70)

Most of the teachers of religion have adopted artificial methods for developing certain spiritual conditions in an aspirant but it is a very defective process. For example, in order to practise *gyan* (gnosticism) and create within the aspirant the state of *Aham Brahmasmi* (I am Brahma) they advise him to meditate outwardly, thinking the same thing all the while and repeating the same words every moment. This is a mechanical process and leads to internal grossness. (p.71)

— ❖ —

By meditation we create a temporary lull in our mind and calmness prevails for the time during which we are in touch with the divine force. But meditation only at a certain fixed hour is not enough, for we are thus in touch with the sacred thought only for a while after which we have no idea of God whatsoever and are for most part of the day away from the path of service and devotion. This is the reason why often after years of practice we still find ourselves at the lowest level of spiritual attainment. What, in fact, we feel during meditation is only simplicity and calmness, if we are rightly guided by a capable master. But an aspirant is generally unable to understand it, for it is beyond his conception at the early stages. The effect thus being imperceptible he often complains that he feels nothing during meditation. This is chiefly due to the fact that he remains in touch with the divine force only for a few minutes of practice. Thus the real thing gained during meditation remains with him only for a while. On the other hand, there is a man who tries to retain the effect gained by meditation for the most part of the day, and abides in the same state for as long as he can. He is, in a way, in constant remembrance of God and his progress is easy and rapid. (p.83)

— ❖ —

During meditation, if you entertain the idea that not you but your Master himself is meditating on his own form, it shall bring about excellent results. Similarly, you can adjust yourself in all your routine of work.

...But those who stick to the idea of the physical form alone as the Master, create for themselves the grossest entanglements and complications. Kabirdas has rightly termed such persons as Guru Pashu. But if the Master is a great divine soul who has secured his merger in absolute Reality, meditation on his form is, by far, of greatest advantage to the disciples. His body, though gross in outward appearance is really as fine and subtle in character as his inner self. If you meditate on the form of such a Master, you not only begin to lose your own grossness but also begin to imbibe within you the finest condition of his inner self. The form taken up in view will after some time disappear from the sight and you will gradually embark on the plane of pure Reality. I have discussed in my book *Commentary on Ten Commandments of Sahaj Marg*, how the form disappears from view when you look at a thing constantly for some time. Thus automatically from the outward form, we travel inwards and then to the real point, where everything disappears. (p.85-86)

— ❖ —

We generally lay stress upon meditation, apparently on human form. The critics may perhaps consider it suicidal to the spiritual feelings. The case is not so, provided the person meditated upon is one of special calibre, who has come down from the Immaterial Absolute for spiritual training, or has attained the spiritual standard of evolution required for the purpose by supreme self-exertion. We take the example of our Master, Samarth Guru Mahatma Shri Ram Chandraji Maharaj of Fatehgarh, U.P. The thing will soon come to light, and the world will remember him ever after. He was one with Nature. If we meditate upon such a great soul, the substance we are seeking for will come by itself. Mathematically, if A is equal to B and C gets equal to A then ultimately C becomes equal to B. If you have selected such a Master as your guide, the problem of life will be easily solved. (p.133)

In raja yoga we generally start with meditation. There is a great underlying philosophy in it. We find ourselves all the time busy with the worldly things. If we are not doing anything, our thoughts seem to have wings in the leisure hours. We are always in tumult and disorder. Our individual mind has become used to such type of character, and thus we have made everything topsy-turvy. Our actions and thoughts count much in our wrong making. When we remain in contact with ideas and thoughts of different kinds, they leave impressions upon our emotional feelings and senses. All senses are spoiled and adopt a wrong course. When such practice continues for a long period, we make them worse. The marks we thus make upon the senses and *indriyas* turn them solid like a rock, having no *bodh* or wisdom. Soul is, no doubt, not acted upon, but we create such obstacles and coverings which keep it enwrapped all round like the cocoon of a silkworm. What happens then? We cannot even peep into the soul, what of realising it. By the effect of our vicious thoughts and actions we spoil our sense of discrimination and right cognition. Those who have reached this state of solidity, as said above, do not like to come under the teaching of raja yoga. This is why people turn a deaf ear to what we say. If somehow or other they make a firm determination to reach the Reality, the power of Master shall affect them. At the same time I want to add that these things can be shattered only by the help of such a Master who has the power of transmission to break open the wrapped-up things and to remove complexities. Of course the abhyasi is directed to have meditation on certain points of concentration, I mean on one of the *chakras*, figuratively called lotuses.

We generally take the heart for meditation. The heart is the pumping station of the blood. It sends out blood, after purification, to different nerves and cells of the body. Now we have taken the heart as the centre of meditation. The blood that runs throughout our system is affected. The solidity due to our own thoughts and actions begins to melt away. This is the first thing we begin to gain, from the very first day, by this method of meditation on the heart. People may ask why it is necessary to proceed with meditation at the first stage of raja yoga. The answer is quite plain and simple. We are now gathering ourselves at one point so that our individual mind may leave its habit of wandering about, which it has formed. By this practice we set our individual mind on the right path because it is now metamorphosing its habit. When this is done our thoughts naturally do not go astray.

It is a Hindu belief, and a correct one too, that when we first came into being we were complete, and we were all in close touch with the Almighty. As time went on degeneration set in with the result that we now find ourselves in the lower stratum of humanity. Who created these things within us? It is only we ourselves and nobody else. It is we who have undermined ourselves; it is we who have thrown ourselves into the gloomy dungeon, far far away from the Godly kingdom; it is we who have wrought this havoc within us, making thereby a network interwoven by the fibres of our wrong and vicious thoughts.

Now we want to go back through downward motion to the condition from which we had come down. We use our central force at one point just as the Almighty did when He created the world by issuing forth the powers of creation from just beneath the Centre through the force of His will, in different forms and colours like the fibres of the net, to complete the creation. It was one with Him when there was no creation. He has been at His centre and shall be there when the things, which have come down, go back in Him, or to the original point called the Centre (as explained later in the book). We began to weave our own fibres of different hues and colours and we are all the time with them. Now we want to return to our own centre. The process naturally will be to draw these things to the point of origin. We do the same thing in meditation and try to gather ourselves at one and the same point to create our *pralaya*, which is the state we were in when we came down.

By meditation we make a will in our heart covering thereby the surroundings around the heart region. It begins to expand, extending over to all *chakras* (lotuses) located in our body. Thus all the *chakras* begin to glow. The circle goes onward passing through region after region till all begin to be absorbed in the innermost circle. What you feel there is dazzling light sometimes, because you have made the passage from the heart towards that region where you are now. The dazzling light now begins to fade because you are going forward. You come in contact with different stages of *maya* as well. The dazzling light is there. When you cross it you find yourself in a totally calm atmosphere. Here the kingdom of God begins. There are stages and stages after it which all pass through. Since it seems out of place to discuss them here under the head of Meditation we leave them aside.

Now your meditation is leading you to the main goal. No practice of hatha yoga can bring about such a result. It fails after *agya chakra*. Meditation—a part of raja yoga—is the only thing that can lead you to the end. There is no other means of approaching the Centre. We have seen that one thought arising out of the Centre created so big a universe. We have got within us the same central force, though marred by our wrong doings. We utilize the same power which is automatic in us. We take work from the same force through meditation. This is how we proceed naturally and with Nature's force, so to say.

When we meditate, the central power we have remains in force. It disperses the overwhelming clouds which are greatly fried up by its force. Only an abhyasi can feel it. This can only be known practically. You will soon find yourself swimming in everlasting peace and happiness. Everything ends here. There is no attachment with the world. The mind is disciplined. It is automatically regulated. Senses begin to come under control, and you gain mastery over them. To master yourself means to master Nature. When the passage becomes clear you feel the Nature's work within your bounds and limits, rather you begin to work yourself. (p.135-138)

Meditation is the foundation of spirituality. If you meditate having your real goal before you, you are sure to arrive at the destination. (p.173)

— ❖ —

The process we start with, and which we lay stress upon, is meditation upon the heart under the guidance of the force of one's master who has attained perfection, and has within him the capacity of transmission. Such a master keeps away things barring our spiritual growth. Spiritual waves from the master continue to flow into our hearts making us calmer and calmer day by day. If we are deep-rooted in meditation, we connect our link with the innermost thing desired. Devotion of course increases the capacity and smoothens the way. If we make our heart the target of masterly force we begin to expand inside, with the result that in the long run we find ourselves stretching throughout the Godly empire. (p.175)

— ❖ —

During our march to freedom we come across various *chakras* having different forms and colours. They are all in the region of heart. Above it the condition is different from what you have already experienced. *Chakras* are all gone. The structure falls off as soon as you proceed onwards. By meditation under the guidance of a capable master the thing becomes easily accessible. Iron will and constant impatience and restlessness for gaining the object bring easy success. (p.176)

— ❖ —

Performing of *sandhya* before sunrise is stressed upon for the reason that the external heat and other influences, which have been driven out of the body, may not creep in again by the effect of the sun which would prevent our deriving the best advantage of the time. It has been generally advised—and Western culture too supports the view—that a separate place must be reserved for each type of work so that relevant thoughts conducive to the nature of the work may spring up on arriving at the place. Man possesses power which he has derived from his thought connection with the Reality. When one resolves to do a thing, the connecting link between the thought and the work becomes intensified, and one begins to draw power from the real source in accordance with the strength of his thought. When the power begins to flow in, and we associate it with a particular point of time, then the remembrance of the work begins to revive in our heart and we begin to feel attached to it in some way or the other. The room or place we sit in for meditation is also charged by our thought force and a feeling of sanctity begins to prevail all over there. The influence taken in by the place helps us further in the accomplishment of the task. Now it depends upon one's individual capacity to expand it as much as he can. It has been generally observed, and the sacred shrines are a living proof of it, that this influence is not exhausted with the lapse of time, and even today pilgrims and visitors get benefited by it. Not only this, since the air blows through, it carries its fragrance to the adjoining layers also. Now there is contraction and expansion in each layer, so the effect thus caused continues to develop and expand. (p.196-197)

— ❖ —

Under Sahaj Marg system of training we start from *dhyan*, the seventh step of Patanjali yoga, fixing our mind on one point in order to practise meditation. The previous steps are not taken up separately but they automatically come into practice as we proceed on with meditation. Thus much of our time and labour are saved. In certain *sansthas* the usual routine followed for practice is often kept confidential. It is released and revealed only to those who undertake to join them formally. What their purpose at the bottom may be, is not quite understandable. Nature has no secrets and I think that one professing to follow the divine path must also have none.

The practice followed in our Mission is meditation on the heart. The same method has been recommended by Patanjali. There is a great philosophy underlying it. We find ourselves all the time busy with worldly things. If we are not doing anything, our thoughts seem to have wings in the leisure hours. We are always in tumult and disorder. Our individual mind has become used to such a characteristic activity, and thus we have made every thing topsy-turvy. Our actions and thoughts count much in our wrong doing. When we remain in contact with ideas and thoughts of different kinds, they leave impressions upon our emotive feelings and senses. All the senses are spoiled and adopt a wrong course. The marks we thus make upon the senses and *indriyas* turn them solid like rock, having no *bodh* or wisdom. Soul is, no doubt, not acted upon, but we create such obstacles and coverings as to keep it enwrapped all round like a cocoon. We cannot even peep into the soul, let alone realising it. By the effect of our vicious thoughts and actions we spoil our sense of discrimination and right cognition. Those who have reached this state of solidity do not like to come under the training course of raja yoga. This is why people turn a deaf ear to what we say.

No practice of hatha yoga can bring out true realisation as it fails after the *ajna chakra* and there still remain very many states still to pass after it. Therefore raja yoga is the only thing that can lead to the end. There is no other means for approaching the Centre. We have got within us the same central force, though marred by our wrong doings. We take work from the same force during meditation. This is how we proceed naturally with nature's force, so to say. When we meditate, the central power we have, remains in force. It disperses the overwhelming clouds which are greatly fried up by its force. It cannot be expressed in words, only an abhyasi can feel it. This can only be known practically. You will soon find yourself swimming in everlasting peace and happiness. Everything ends here. There remains no attachment with the world. The mind is disciplined, it is regulated automatically. Senses begin to come under control and you gain mastery over them. To master yourself means to master

Nature. When the passage becomes clear you find Nature's work within your bounds and limits: rather you begin to work yourself.

In our system the abhyasi is advised to meditate on the heart thinking of the divine light there. But he is directed not to view light in any form or shape like that of an electric bulb or a candle, etc. In that case the light appearing therein will not be real, but one projected by his own creative speculation. An abhyasi is advised to proceed with a mere supposition of light with the thought of Divinity at the bottom. What happens then is that we meditate upon the subtlest which is to be attained.

The method of meditation on the heart is to think of Godly light within it. When you begin meditating in this way please think only that Godly light within is attracting you. Do not mind if extraneous ideas haunt you during meditation. Let them come but go on with your own work. Treat your thoughts and ideas as uninvited guests. If even then they trouble you think they are Master's, not yours. This process of meditation is very effective, and can never fail in bringing about the desired result. Sit in an easy posture for an hour in the morning in quite a natural way. You should only meditate. You should not struggle with your ideas which generally come during meditation. (p.340-342)

— ❖ —

When the thought of going back to the original was stirred up in man, it became essential for him to bring activity, which had sprung up in him into a latent state as far as it was possible. He began to seek out means for it. At last it came to his understanding that just as the latent motion was grosser in comparison to the Absolute with which it was connected, even so he must take up something grosser for the purpose, to enable him to attain the desired ideal of Reality. This led him to the conclusion that he must create in him a form of contraction or withdrawal similar to that at the time of *pralaya*. Now Self is all pervading in man just as it is in the whole universe—taking the universe in a collective sense. The state of *pralaya* comes in when contraction begins to take place. Similar contraction in man leads to his individual *pralaya*. That means that he begins to proceed from his state of grossness to the real state. The contraction always starts from below and proceeds gradually upwards because of its upward tendency. Therefore, in order to go upwards he must start contracting from below. The form of contraction could be only to bring his legs and allied parts to one pose and to keep them steady. In whatever way it might be done, the form will finally be that of the *asan*. It is essential because it paves our way to the Ultimate. This posture must always be the same. The reason is that in this way he gets himself associated with the great power, the very thing he takes up in the beginning for the attainment of his particular objective. Thus the form which is associated with Reality helps him a good deal in his primary initiation.

The upright position of the back-bone, neck and head in an erect straight line during meditation has been thought to be most advantageous from very ancient times, because the flow of Divine grace is believed to descend straight upon the abhyasi in that posture. In our way of practice, however, this is not insisted upon. I advise the abhyasis generally to sit in a natural easy posture. Moreover, even those who assume a tight straight pose, are found to give way automatically to a suppliant, slightly forward drooping posture, as the state of blissful absorbency sets in. As such, it may be considered to be more natural even for the purpose of an ascent into higher states of consciousness. In fact a controversy over a point of comparatively lesser significance seems irrelevant.

It is better to sit in the grey of the morning for meditation, or when that is not possible, at any fixed hour convenient to the abhyasi. Do not feel disturbed with the outer things but remain engaged with your own work thinking that they are in a way helping you to feel the necessity for greater absorption in your practice. (p.346-348)

Complete Works of Ram Chandra, Volume II
Shri Ram Chandra

People hanker after peace; so how can they be induced to take up restless longing for the realisation of the object? I may assure you that the charms of this restlessness are far greater than those of peace. Peace which people talk about may no doubt be a high attainment, of which an abhyasi experiences a taste during meditation. But that also reveals that there must be a central point of it. (p.4)

— ❖ —

As a general rule one does not feel much interested in meditation when the cleaning process is being effected, or when impressions and bondages are being loosened, which is in fact the only effective course and one greatly helpful to his sacred cause. But while I proceed on thus, I have to make allowance for his craving for peace and satisfaction as well, which he wishes for and values most. For this reason when he does not feel interested in meditation while receiving this type of transmission from me, he thinks it to be of no avail and consequently drops off from satsangh. The proper course should have been that after having judged fully the capability of the teacher and finding him quite up to the mark, he should trust him and follow him, leaving everything to him. He should not dictate terms for the ways and lines for his spiritual training, because the teacher alone can understand what is best for the abhyasi.

Often, some of the abhyasis complain that during their individual practice they do not have the same amount of calmness and absorption as they have while sitting with me. That is but natural, since their main objective is the attainment of peace and not of realisation. Besides if I take the privilege of asking them how long and how often they practise at home, it will be clear that in most of the cases they do not practise even for an aggregate period of one hour during a whole week. Certain *sansthas* advise meditation for six hours a day or even more, with the rest of the time devoted to satsangh, whereas I advise only for an hour in the morning and another hour in the evening. But even for this they offer excuses saying that they do not get time, or they do not feel absorbed during meditation. They can however discover the reason themselves. But if they like I can tell them that this is due to lack of interest and devotion in them. If one feels inwardly devoted to God, meditation becomes a part of his duty and then there is no question of inclination or lack of absorption.

Often people put forward excuses for not being regular with their practice of meditation, saying that they are faced with worries, troubles and engagements. They mean thereby that they can continue their practice of meditation only when they are free from all distractions. What they really expect is that I should exercise my power or will to extricate them from out of their worries and troubles and set them on the path. Then alone will they be prepared to follow and practise. (p.11-12)

— ❖ —

He [Lalaji] advised meditation on the heart as the easiest method and this is followed in the Mission. Meditation on certain other points such as the tip of the nose or the mid-point between the two eyebrows, as advised elsewhere, may also serve to some extent, but in my opinion meditation on the heart is the easiest and the most efficacious. I have sufficiently dealt with this point in the *Efficacy of Raja Yoga*. We have so far been extroverts but now we have to become introverts by turning our mind inwards. When we are successful in our efforts we automatically begin to have spiritual experiences, and our march on the path of spirituality goes on without interruption. Other forms of *sadhana* may also perhaps be helpful to some extent, but this at least is quite certain that so long as we are extroverts our eye can never turn inwards. The most helpful methods would therefore be only those which are quite simple and natural, and free from all grosser effects. (p.45-46)

There are certain *granthis* or knots in all regions. When the current of Nature flowed down from the Origin to effect creation, the jerks created knots which became centres of power. In the course of our swimming up through these currents, the knots begin to get unfolded through the power of meditation, making our advance easier and more smooth. (p.46)

— ❖ —

If we think ourselves to be the lover and Him as the Beloved and proceed on with the same feeling, the course would be easier. The result that will follow in due course would be, that God himself shall become the lover and we the beloved. This is really the fourth stage of meditation. But if we think at this stage that we have realised the Goal, it is a blunder. Much remains ahead still. (p.48)

— ❖ —

The method of meditation on the heart is to think of the Godly light within it. When you begin meditation in this way please think once only that Godly light within is attracting you. Do not mind if extraneous ideas intrude during meditation. Let them come, but you go on with your own work. Sit in an easy posture for one hour in the morning in quite a natural way. If you require the philosophy of this method I shall reveal it to you after some time. You should only meditate. You should not struggle with the ideas and thoughts which generally come in during meditation. Concentration is the result of meditation. Those who want concentration for the sake of meditation and force their mind to it generally meet with failure. It must be remembered that while practising these methods one should not force his mind too much, but only sit in a normal way. Sit in an easy posture for one hour in the morning, in quite a natural way. It is better to sit in the grey of the morning for meditation or, if that is not possible, then at any fixed hour convenient to you, the abhyasi. Do not feel disturbed by the outer things but remain engaged with your work, thinking that they are in a way helping you to feel the necessity of greater absorption in your practice. (p.66-67)

— ❖ —

My Master was everything to me as He is today. I meditated upon his form within my heart and outside as well. But I do not recommend this to you for you have not seen him. The benefit I derived from this process is beyond words to describe. Some people may have objection to it though the 37th Sutra of Patanjali's 'Yoga Darshana' fully supports it. (*Vitaragavishayam va chittam* I.37) I am not at all in favour of meditation on the pictures of saints. (p.69)

— ❖ —

The basis of meditation is purely spiritual, while that of concentration is only the ego. When you mean to concentrate, 'you' are there, quite definitely, but when you meditate, you wait for something higher, hence you are away from the idea of self.

The only proper course for an aspirant would therefore be to get himself absorbed in the light of the Divine coming to him from the Original source, without minding the implications of the word concentration. In that case the question of concentration will not arise at all, and one will all along be with that which can neither be interpreted as concentration nor otherwise. Concentration with all its implications affecting enclosement, being not of any avail, it is only the power of 'non-concentration' as I may call it that enables one's approach to higher and higher regions of enlightenment. Proceeding along in that way, one would keep on imbibing the power of the Source to light himself up with Divine effulgence.

Now what condition does the word 'non-concentration' refer to? Obviously it refers to a state associated with an overflow of thoughts. But then there are two aspects of it: the one when the flow is not conjoined with our conscious knowledge, and the other when we have a conscious awareness of it, and take its effect upon the mind. This, the latter one, may no doubt amount to a state of distraction, especially when one is linked with the thought of some misery or affliction. In the former case, though the flow continues uninterruptedly, yet the encumbering effect thereof is not felt upon the mind. Normally this state of mind is seldom found to be disturbing. Taking these two aspects into view I might say that the latter is quite similar to the state known as concentration, but with only this difference that here the object of concentration is one's distraction and worry instead of the godly thought. It may therefore be taken as crude concentration which is maintained by the force of our unconscious efforts. The effect in both the cases (viz., by conscious effort and by unconscious effort) is the same i.e., heaviness, dullness, sluggishness. The very word concentration implies a sense of artificiality, and effort is for that reason indispensable. When the flow of thought is spontaneous it is effortless and closely similar to the state commonly known as concentration. The proper word for that may therefore be 'absorption', which is a natural course and follows by itself as the result of meditation on the right lines.

Concentration taken in the sense of absorption (non-concentration, with flow of thoughts, without effect on the mind) is the real state. It may be of different types at different levels. One may be the concentration of the lower level, another that of the higher level, and still another that of the highest level. Now taking out the common factor 'concentration' from these, what remains thereafter is only the lower, the higher and the highest. That is how one has to go on with his march towards the Ultimate. On the other hand if our thought remains involved with the idea of concentration, the inner force will not be working actively to offer us impetus for our higher ascent. The proper course would therefore be to take up the thought in the form of *sankalpa* (subtle idea) without any imposed resolve or effort, and proceed on with it in a gentle and natural way without enforcing any artificiality or imposition. Such is the process followed in Sahaj Marg which, as a matter of fact, introduces through the

Master's *pranahuti* from the very beginning that very state which lies at the farthest end. Though in the beginning one might have, at times, only glimpses of it, yet after continued practice the same condition covers him all over. This is why in spite of the continuity of thoughts often present at the time of meditation, one proceeding by Sahaj Marg experiences a peculiar state of concentration better interpreted as 'absorption'. (p.75-77)

— ❖ —

Under Sahaj Marg the Divine grace is directed towards the abhyasi through the process of *pranahuti.* As a matter of fact what *pranahuti* does for the spiritual uplift of the abhyasi in the shortest possible time, independent efforts cannot do even in a full decade. Serious difficulties often arise when meditation is practised independently in accordance with the old methods prescribed in books. Under the old system of abhyas one has to keep on struggling with the mind in order to stop its unceasing activities. The struggle continues all the time without any success in the real sense. Thus practically there is no meditation at all, and all the time is lost in mere struggling and suppressing mental modifications. In order to overcome this very great difficulty, under the Sahaj Marg system we simply connect ourselves with the power of the Master whose mind has become thoroughly disciplined and regulated. His power then begins to flow into the individual regulating his mental tendencies. (p.86-87)

— ❖ —

So far as my personal experience goes, I find in most of them a rock-like solidity firmly settled in their hearts. They are generally those who adhere rigidly to the worship of idols and images. In certain cases I have discovered peculiar types of folds and creases in their hearts, which are mostly due to the effect of wrong methods of meditation or concentration practised by them. The most appropriate points for meditation can only be those from where the current flows on either upwards or downwards. It can only be either the heart or the *trikuti* (centre between eyebrows). Meditation on the point of the navel has no spiritual value, except that it causes a tickling sensation which finally excites the mind and makes the passions all the more powerful. (p.118-119)

— ❖ —

Treat your thoughts and ideas as uninvited guests. If they trouble you further just imagine them to be mine and not yours. This process is very effective and can never fail to bring about the desired result. Please inform me of the results. Thoughts can be stopped just in a moment, but that will not be in our interest since for the attainment of liberation it is but essential to throw out the buried thoughts after having completed their *bhoga.*

...You can meditate for any length of time but there must not be any mental exhaustion. (p.121)

— ❖ —

...our thought travels on towards the ultimate. This we develop by the practice of meditation. When we begin doing it, help begins to flow down from the very source. When you link yourself with it, the outer charms begin to fade automatically. It is good that you have made up your mind for abhyas, but its fulfillment also rests upon you alone. If you take in a deep impression of the Reality, meditation cannot but start by itself.

Thank God you have started *puja* (meditation); otherwise I would have considered it as my own weakness. When you have started meditation, I am sure "the eye of the bubble will soon witness the face of water." May God grant you perseverance and steadiness. You say that some particular force takes hold of your body, pushing aside other forces and makes you do the abhyas. Thank God you have begun to receive my transmission. My prayer is now proving to be fruitful. You may consider it a good sign for your progress. When it is so, I find no reason why you should not have a taste of the state of absorbency and of the feeling of light. (p.126)

— ❖ —

I always tried to see the whole physical form of the Master in my vision, and during meditation I always meditated upon his form, placing it within my heart. (p.144)

— ❖ —

Fickle-mindedness has become part and parcel of our life, because we have directed the individual mind towards that course. The case was not so when we came first into the world. The surroundings, environment, and our habits caused their own effect with the result that we got completely spoiled. But as a matter of fact we alone are responsible for all this. Therefore it now rests upon us to bring it round again to the proper course. It is for this alone that we practise meditation to relieve the mind of its wandering tendency. (p.147)

— ❖ —

The only effective instrument for avoiding a fall is meditation on the form of the Master, a Master in the true sense of course. The process shall be much helpful in securing synonymity which is one of the highest attainments on the path, and may be interpreted as an advanced state of mergence. (p.155)

— ❖ —

I am not opposed to *japa* but I do not approve of the ways in which it is generally practised. ... For example, *gayatri japa* is one of the essential features of general *sadhana* and is practised by most, irrespective of other *japas* which might have been advised at times. The way in which it should be done is as follows. The abhyasi is to sit in a meditative mood, repeating the mantra mentally twice or thrice, keeping in view the sense it conveys. He is then to begin meditating upon the sense. The words will naturally go out of his consciousness and the thought alone will remain in his mind. After some time when he gets absorbed in it, the thought too shall vanish and nothing shall remain except absorbency in the prayerful mood. That is the proper way. (p.166-167)

— ❖ —

As a matter of fact the process indirectly involves meditation on the form of the Master. As such it is quite necessary that the form taken up for the purpose must be of one of the highest calibre endowed with all the greatest moral and spiritual values. In that case the process will help the development of similar virtues in the abhyasi. The scientific principle underlying this process is that when an abhyasi meditates his thoughts create a vacuum in his heart which begins to be filled up with the power of that which is meditated upon, so as to keep up the balance in accordance with the law of Nature. So long as it persists, the power continues to flow in automatically. (p.196-197)

— ❖ —

The technique of Sahaj Marg ... prescribes meditation on the heart, supposing the presence of Divine light there. But the abhyasi is directed not to try to see the light in any form or shape. If he does so the light, if perchance it appears to his view, will not be the real one but a projection of his mind. An abhyasi is, however, advised to take it in the form of mere supposition. In that case it will be the subtlest, and we shall thereby be meditating upon the subtlest. Every saint has used the word Light for it and I too cannot avoid it, since that is the only expression best suited for the purpose. But that creates some complications, because when we talk of light the idea of luminosity becomes predominant, and we begin to take it as glittering. The real light carries with it no such sense and may be represented as 'light without luminosity.' (p.211)

Barking of dogs refers to the unregulated activities of the mind and the *indriyas* which can easily be set right by meditation and remembrance. (p.232)

— ❖ —

Numerous ways are prescribed for securing Realisation, each one suited to a particular taste or mentality of the individual. A man of the lowest standard, who cannot give his mind up to meditation, may however, on account of his inner grossness, take the solid things to start with and begin worshipping images with the *bhava* of Almighty of course. (p.236)

— ❖ —

He thus acquires the state of *nishkam karma*, so beautifully discussed by Lord Krishna in the Gîta. At this stage the man attains an almost balanced state similar to that which prevailed before the creation came into existence. His heart is quite calm, and the mind disciplined. He is so much absorbed in *Brahm* that he does not like to part with it even for a moment. So he can no longer meditate either on God or on himself. If, however, he attempts to meditate for a while, breathlessness will follow, since he is swimming in the sphere where there is no density. At this stage they say that self is realised... (p.258)

— ❖ —

Generally I advise meditation on the heart at the point where you feel its beatings. I do not want to expand its vision to the whole of the region of the heart. Therefore, an abhyasi is to know the heart as said above, to meditate upon. The points 'A' and 'B' are also the other points for meditation but I have not prescribed them for all as they are unnecessary at the initial stage. We must satisfy our thirst by drinking the water and not by brooding over the cause of it. I have divided the heart into two parts, not dwelling upon its details which are to be understood practically by means of abhyas. (p.264)

Like my Master I do not make compulsion for anything except meditation, but I am obliged to say that they do not feel even this incumbent upon them to follow it. (p.286)

— ❖ —

A man just enters the spiritual life. Call him as A.

...A finds B as a greater personality who can weave his destiny. He now begins to love B. ...A treats B as God and forms, on account of intense love, his image in his own heart. He does not want to be away from the thought for even a moment. He craves the great personality in his heart. In other words, he keeps his ideal safe in his bosom. What torments him much is B's funny play just as a child when it grows old, hides himself under the clothes of his mother and tells her to seek him. Suppose the child's mother has no covering? Where then will the child hide himself? A is meditating on B and the cover comes in itself and the image seems hidden. Where does this covering come from? It is the veil of his own thought which has kept him aloof from his great Master—the Almighty. (p.286-287)

— ❖ —

...while you are meditating think that your Master is himself meditating on his own form. (p.289)

— ❖ —

Go on doing the process of meditation till it is matured. This is the last stage of meditation. When we become one with the real thing, the things following it grow so dark that we do not perceive them. In other words, we become blind in this respect and our vision for the real things improves and we bring it to such a standard that we are lost altogether. (p.305)

What a nice philosophy is contained in the saying that everything appears as round. The reason is that when That Great Architect willed to create the universe and used the energy, the actions started in a round way in order to establish a circuit so that the energy could work. Even as when you transmit, your energy also works in a circuit so that the abhyasi may be affected. And we sit for meditation making a circle of the satsanghis, because this too may help us. (p.317-318)

— ❖ —

Centre is God Himself; the Master cell and all other cells are His creation. If anybody tries to meditate upon the Centre his efforts will not be successful, though in his imagination he may however take the Centre in view to meditate upon. The only way for that would be the one I have hinted at in the book *Anant-Ki-Or* (*Towards Infinity*), but I forbid every body to attempt it. I had attempted it twice with prayers to the Master, only for two or three seconds each time. Because of the immense power there, on the border ring, I had myself put a strong check over my heart and at the same time the Master's powerful hand was also there. Even then I could only peep into it but not meditate upon it at all, because the pressure on the heart was unbearably great. (p.333)

When you feel unable to meditate on the form in any way, you may just suppose that the form is before you. When this too cannot be done, that trend of meditation will itself be revealed. (p.357)

— ❖ —

It happens that sometimes during meditation the abhyasi feels absorbed, while sometimes he does not. The reason is that the samskaras which are firmly rooted in their 'field' come towards the heart to go out. This is because meditation creates a vacuum in the heart. As long as all samskaras are not thrown out, there cannot be Liberation. As a matter of fact I go on cleaning them in the routine course also. ...

Whatever condition develops during meditation, whether it is liked by the abhyasi or disliked, is beneficial in every way.

(p.375)

The Autobiography of Ram Chandra, Volume I
Shri Ram Chandra

I started meditation not on Divine light as is prescribed in the Shri Ram Chandra Mission, but on my Master's form, seeing Him in my heart. This was quite spontaneous and automatic, and I went on with it.

I sincerely took up the method of meditation after I passed the S.S.L.C. and Matriculation examination. Within six months, I saw in meditation that the whole of my heart was filled with soothing light, and a plant full of light was emitting forth light from all its branches and leaves. I continued practice. Six months later, I noticed a peculiar thing in my heart, that my heart was reciting the word 'Om'. This we call *ajapa.* (p.20-21)

— ❖ —

As I said before, I started meditation upon His form within my heart. In the beginning the form remains in view but after some time the vision begins to fade away, till only a reflection, *aakaar*, remains. This too melts away after some time and only an idea of it remains. Besides this, I used to meditate upon His complete form placed before me. The subsequent stages involved in the process are also similar. After some practice the form grows subtler and subsequently begins to fade away, leaving in its place a mere idea of it. When that too disappears, the abhyasi should take it as a mere supposition that it is there. Later on, when that supposition too vanishes, there comes the second stage. But this must come naturally and automatically, and not by willed effort to create this condition. At this stage the abhyasi begins to feel himself as the Master. If he is sensitive enough, he then begins to feel that all parts of his body, limbs, etc., are those of the Master. Here again I shall repeat the same warning that this must also develop naturally and automatically, and not by willed effort. If the abhyasi goes along in the correct manner, the body idea will soon begin to vanish. He will begin to feel that the body is neither his nor of the Master. But still he should have the idea that his body is that of the Master. When that idea vanishes, he should suppose that he is the Master. In the end, when the supposition also fades away, the process will bring itself to the third stage—that is the soul within the Master. This will complete all steps automatically, after which there remains neither the idea of the body nor of the soul. He is nowhere now, and the task is practically over. When I was in this last state of meditation on Soul, I was asked by my Master in a dream to meditate on the soul itself and He told me the process also which was as below:

"Lie down straight upon the bed without movement and meditate upon soul for some time."

I did it for a full month, taking leave from the office in order to devote maximum time to it. It was all due to the Grace of my Master, and Master alone, that this process came to my mind automatically—each step itself giving a clue to the next step.

Of course my Master never asked anybody to meditate upon His form, and I am proud that I was the only person who adopted this process though there were many others who used to have His remembrance off and on. (p.24-26)

— ❖ —

...in meditation you wait for something and that is God. Waiting produces a sort of attraction automatically on account of continuous effort. (p.30)

In the morning there was uneasiness which lasted for half an hour.

Going beyond easiness is uneasiness. A man becomes conscious when similarity or sameness is disturbed. As long as easiness is there, there is no disturbance. The state we acquire by the help of the meditation causes a repulse. When the outgoing tendencies of the mind come in touch with it or, in other words, when the tendencies touch the field of easiness, its opposite is felt. So we should also try to calm down the outgoing tendencies of the mind. (p.43)

— ❖ —

I dreamt that a holy personality asked me to sit down and transmitted to me. I woke up, and after this I kept on sitting in meditation for some time.

After years of practice when the meditation grows deeper and the thought begins to start one's upward march, one comes to a point where one feels "I am the power myself." It happens when *surat* comes in contact with glimpses of the Divine. It loses its own character and gains the Divine one. There one starts to feel "I am Brahman." I give the meaning of *surat* in this way. When thought comes in contact with soul, a third thing, a spark, is produced. This is termed *surat*. It leads to the Highest. Thoughts lag behind. They have no accommodation in the sphere of divinity. (p.44-45)

The Autobiography of Ram Chandra, Volume II
Shri Ram Chandra

Lalaji confirmed that meditation on Master's form would prove immensely beneficial, provided that the Master has merged himself totally in the Ultimate. (p.14)

"One thing which should never be forgotten is that if there is any defect, either internal or external, in the trainer, it will be transmitted into the abhyasi also who meditates on the form of the trainer. That is why meditation should be done only on the form of one whose disposition is completely balanced, and who is free from those defects which are considered to be undesirable in spirituality, or which are detrimental to a moral life. I think every abhyasi should not be told about meditation on the form unless the trainer himself has attained that condition." [Lalaji]

(p.41)

— ❖ —

"There is an indecent thing which my disciples generally do. They take the portion of the head alone for meditation whereas the full form should be taken. You have done the correct thing. Still you felt dissatisfied. You always thought that you could not practise meditation on right lines. All your limitations have been broken." [Lalaji] (p.49)

— ❖ —

A method to reduce the bustles and struggle of the mind (which is thrown out of balance): "The active condition of the mind is mostly in the heart. The mind should be considered as a part of the Ultimate in such a way that both of them are of the same colour. By colour is not meant red, yellow, black and so on, but that if the Ultimate is light (as it has been called or described), mind also is a like part of it. The tendency of the mind should be drawn towards the Ultimate in such a way that the mind is meditating, as it were, on the Ultimate. This thought should be maintained during the transmission as long as one gives the sitting. All the complaints of the mind will be set right by this method." [Lalaji] (p.69)

Messages Universal
Shri Ram Chandra

This wonderful process which is based on spiritual science is of immense value to an abhyasi. In my case the process started by itself. As a matter of fact the process indirectly involves meditation on the form of the Master. As such it is quite necessary that the form taken up for the purpose must be of one of the highest calibre endowed with all the greatest moral and spiritual values. In that case the process will help development of similar virtues in the abhyasi. The scientific principle underlying this process is that when an abhyasi meditates his thoughts create a vacuum in his heart which begins to be filled up with the power of that which is meditated upon, so as to keep up the balance in accordance with the law of Nature. So long as it persists, the power continues to flow in automatically. (p.3-4)

— ❖ —

One thing which I like to introduce in our satsangh is that at 9:00 p.m. sharp every abhyasi, wherever he might happen to be at the time, should stop his work and meditate for fifteen minutes, thinking that all brothers and sisters are being filled up with love and devotion and that real faith is growing stronger in them. It shall be of immense value to them, which their practical experience only shall reveal. (p.6)

— ❖ —

He advised meditation on the heart as the easiest method and this is followed in the Mission. Meditation on certain other points such as the tip of the nose or the mid-point between the two eyebrows, as advised elsewhere, may also serve to some extent, but in my opinion meditation on the heart is the easiest and the most efficacious. I have sufficiently dealt with this point in the *Efficacy of Raja Yoga*. We have so far been extroverts but now we have to become introverts by turning our mind inwards.

When we are successful in our efforts we automatically begin to have spiritual experiences, and our march on the path of spirituality goes on without interruption. Other forms of *sadhana* may also perhaps be helpful to some extent, but this at least is quite certain that so long as we are extroverts our eye can never turn inwards.

The most helpful methods would therefore be only those which are quite simple and natural, and free from all grosser effects. For acquiring *that* which is the subtlest beyond all possible limits, we must naturally be attracted towards means which tend to make us the lightest and the subtlest. (p.20-21)

— ❖ —

If we think ourselves to be the lover and Him as the Beloved and proceed on with the same feeling, the course would be easier. The result that will follow in due course would be, that God himself shall become the lover and we the beloved. This is really the fourth stage of meditation. But if we think at this stage that we have realised the Goal, it is a blunder. (p.25)

— ❖ —

The practices advised under the system are not merely formal and mechanical, related with the closing of eyes for meditation. They have a definite object, a purpose and an end. (p.40)

— ❖ —

The routine practice followed in our sanstha is meditation on the heart. The same practice has also been advised by Patanjali. The basic principle of this process has already been discussed in the *Efficacy of Raja Yoga*, which I do not mean to repeat here again.

...The technique of Sahaj Marg, though quite simple, is often beyond common grasp, since it adheres closely to the absolute Reality and proceeds along subtlest lines. It prescribes meditation on the heart, supposing the presence of Divine light there. But the abhyasi is directed not to try to see the light in any form or shape. If he does see the light, if perchance it appears to his view, it will not be the real one but a projection of his mind. An abhyasi is, however, advised to take it in the form of mere supposition. In that case it will be the subtlest, and we shall thereby be meditating upon the subtlest. Every saint has used the word Light for it and I too cannot avoid it, since that is the only expression best suited for the purpose. But that creates some complications, because when we talk of light the idea of luminosity becomes predominant, and we begin to take it as glittering. The real light carries with it no such sense and may be represented as 'light without luminosity'. It refers to the very real substance or, more appropriately, the substance which is associated with neither light nor darkness but is beyond both.

Under our system of practice too, an abhyasi no doubt does see the light sometimes, but that is only in the beginning when matter comes into contact with energy. In other words it is a clue to show that energy has begun to work. Moreover light not being our goal, the vision of luminosity within or without is not an indication of the attainment of Realisation. (p.44-46)

— ❖ —

I have already mentioned about the forces of Nature and the power arcs. They are all utilised for the transformation of man in the way it is required. We proceed with meditation on the heart thinking of the Divine light within, and by so doing we gradually begin to rise or to express it better, to dive deep into the inner consciousness, with the result that an abhyasi begins to feel expansion, this being the first phase. That means we have sown the seed of Infinity, or in other words we have revived the thing which had slipped from our view. (p.62)

In our Sahaj Marg system a teacher takes out the hurdles in the progress of the seeker and side by side imparts the divine effulgence in him, which if an abhyasi does it himself takes hundreds of years and often fails to clean his system. We start with the meditation upon heart, taking the object of meditation as subtle as possible. Shri Ramanujachari has forbidden meditation on concrete object on the basis of ancient authority. (p.83-84)

— ❖ —

God is the subtlest being and in order to realise Him the subtlest means are the only way. This does not mean that for realising God one has to ignore the needs of physical body or empirical world. If perchance we fall upon the means which go on adding grossness we shall definitely remain away from the vision of Absolute Reality. It is an established fact that meditation is a subtle method provided the object of meditation is not concrete. That is why under Sahaj Marg we advise to meditate supposing the presence of Divine light in the heart. The *Upanishads* also corroborate this. This practice supported by the transmission of Divine effulgence becomes subtler and subtler until it becomes the subtlest. (p.86-87)

— ❖ —

I am happy that all of you follow the meditation prescribed; but there are a few who remain non-attached after the meditation is over. They forget the idea of God and begin to remember themselves throughout the light of the sun. It is their work to shape themselves for the Divine purpose. (p.97)

— ❖ —

In Sahaj Marg, Divine grace is directed toward the abhyasi through the process of *pranahuti* (transmission). As a matter of fact, what *pranahuti* does for the spiritual uplift of an abhyasi and removal of complexities in a short time, independent efforts cannot achieve even in a full decade. Serious difficulties arise when meditation is practised independently in accordance with the old methods prescribed in books. Under the old system, one has to keep on struggling with the mind in order to suppress its unceasing activities. This continues all the time and there is practically no meditation at all and all the time given to meditation is lost in struggling against and trying to suppress thoughts and tendencies.

In order to overcome this greatest difficulty, under the Sahaj Marg, one has simply to connect oneself with the power of the Master whose mind, senses and faculties are all thoroughly disciplined and regulated. This power then begins to flow in regulating the tendencies of the abhyasi's mind also. The Master's help is, therefore, of prime value for sure success.

Usually, people initially aim at the cessation of the activities of the mind. This can best be achieved by linking ourselves with the great power which is beyond the range of senses or in other words, one who has transcended its limits. By connecting ourselves with such a person with love and devotion and by practising meditation in the right manner, we begin to get transformed accordingly. (p.101-103)

— ❖ —

The first and almost immediate effect of the transmission is to give peace and calmness which can hardly be expressed in words. This experience in meditation helps to gently remind us of the source to which we must return and repeated experience strengthens the remembrance of our original home, and so loosens the bondage of the present life. As the transmission takes us to deeper and deeper levels of remembrance, our journey to the source becomes firmly established. (p.106)

— ❖ —

...my Master Samarth Guru Mahatma Shri Ram Chandraji Maharaj of Fatehgarh (U.P.) India, has remodeled the 'Yoga' in a way that somehow you may come into contact with the Divine speedily. The main feature of the system is that we get plenty of help from the Master. Simple meditation is prescribed, which helps all along in the spiritual pursuit. Do not believe anything unless you have tested it. Sahaj Marg is an open chapter for the seekers to have their own experience to believe it. (p.119)

— ❖ —

Before concluding, I would like to say something about the thoughts coming during the meditation for which I receive complaints from many associates from practically all over the country as also from abroad. Thoughts during meditation are just like the children playing on the road. When your attention is not towards thoughts, they are wholly ineffective and are of no value. Actually thoughts do not disturb you, but you yourself feel disturbed. I have very often said that the best way to get rid of them is to be unmindful towards them and treat them as you treat uninvited guests. They rise for the sake of fall. They are leaving their field waiting for the Divinity to come in. When the force of meditation tears off the veil of the heat, these thoughts are attracted because of a little bit of vacuum which is there. When thoughts arise, you feel disturbed, so the thoughts do not meddle with you, rather you meddle with them. (p.147)

— ❖ —

The general idea that fills abhyasis is that the items of practice taught to them are all that is needed to take them up to the final state of evolution. Their thought does not run beyond this at all. We indicate raja yoga as our foundation and it is so in fact, their ideation does not reach down to its depths and it just stops short with the observance of the rules. But it is certain that in Sahaj Marg, the fragrance of *pranahuti* indwells, but still the factors that get left behind are love and devotion. Along with the act of meditation, it is essential that these should also inhere therein. It has been necessary for me to stress the mingling of the facets together, since by doing this the *sadhak* may be able to reach his goal very soon. It is your responsibility to engender these factors in yourselves. (p.150-151)

— ❖ —

Truth lies in this that we keep turning our vision inward; if you do this, your condition will stay there wherefrom the 'Substance' came to us, that is, we make a mark on the true 'Treasure House'. Now it is left to us just to develop the form of expansion. This form of expansion takes birth when, along with practising meditation on the Divine, the endeavour is maintained to keep our vision more and more turning inward. (p.153)

— ❖ —

No doubt the world is in us and we are in the world, but we have to search out who is behind the scene. Meditation and everything is for that alone. We feel He is hiding from us, although it is not the case. We see stars sometime, but after some advancement, we begin to feel the lustre of the sun; and after that there comes the time when we are able to see the sun itself. As long as we think of the lustre of the sun, the real sun remains hidden from our view. I earnestly pray that all may reach the Goal—the cause of all our existence. (p.169)

— ❖ —

The path is cleaner in proportion to our devotion. You receive a push from the heart, while meditating on Him, to impel you on the way. The dirt and refuse are our conflicting ideas. While meditating, if you secure even a temporary lull, that means you have gone a step further on the path. You will find the conflicting ideas disappearing, when you are on your way to the path. When you acquire a state of permanency in your meditation, touching the innermost plane, the idea of the Ultimate or God becomes quite near you. (p.178-179)

Letters of the Master, Volume I—1960 to 1971
[Letters by Babuji to Dr. K.C. Varadachari]

Sit for meditation in the morning, say for half an hour in the beginning and think that Divine light is present in your heart. Do this in quite simple and natural way, without forcing your mind to it. Never mind if you do not actually see the light there. Start with a mere supposition so to say and remain sitting in a meditative mood (in one posture as far as possible) with your inward eye turned towards the heart, in the most natural way, without trying to force yourself to concentrate. (p.9)

— ❖ —

The meditation I have written to you is not to gain anything so that you may develop idolatry but it is for the cleaning of the different forms of idolatry which have entered into being. We do not conceive it as a paraphernalia of *shanti* or bliss so that it may bring artificial trend, but we make it a source to bring the standard of Reality which is yet to dawn. It is not the case here. We are only setting up an equation having X as the value to solve the problem of life. You have expressed in your letter your revolting nature against imagination, etc. I have taken all these points into consideration, before prescribing the meditation to our associates. Sometimes a peculiar meditation, prescribed under the avowed authority, becomes dangerous and my revered Master had strictly warned not to prescribe such meditations unless one has become capable of hitting at the root or the Divine wisdom has developed. I have taken all these precautions while laying down the prescription. (p.61)

— ❖ —

You need not do any meditation during illness. Really speaking you are all the time in meditation inwardly. So please start the meditation when you recover. (p.92)

You are nearly all the time in meditation. So if the duration has not increased it matters little. But if you increase the meditation then you will have the knowledge and experience of your spiritual elevation. (p.114-115)

— ❖ —

If the abhyasi observes minutely he will see that the idea of heart is gone and he is meditating internally on some higher plane. Sometimes he is so much internally connected that he feels the pure divine touch. (p.129)

— ❖ —

I am very glad to see in your letter that you are increasing the duration of the meditation. You have tremendous contact with me even if you do not increase the time you will improve, but if you do so you will gain experience and knowledge. When you sit in meditation the things coming within your purview are polarized as you meditate with the idea of tranquillity and realisation. You will be surprised to know that my associates Dr. P. Sen of Calcutta Medical College meditates for six to eight hours daily. Recently he meditated for ten hours together with the idea of sacrificing his life and to become one with Brahm. He felt sensations at *sahasra dal kamal* and wanted to give up his life through that centre. The result was that he suffered from paralysis of the left hand. He will recover soon. (p.137)

— ❖ —

For your craving to discover and see the states, I suggest the following but it must be done only once or at the most twice.

'Lie down flat on the bed and begin to meditate on your soul.' By the process may you begin to discover the states. But it is rather difficult to understand the finer states of subtle existence. (p.180)

You meditate on the heart waiting for His grace, that means you get into practice in inviting His grace. When this power develops to the highest degree of eminence, the greatest souls can appear before him at his bid. The next thing is when you meditate on light, for reality, the very attribute of God which you have made the point of meditation, brings the real thing at the bottom. So, please, if you feel anything, it must be written to me because feeling will continue. (p.229)

— ❖ —

You will laugh at me if I say that I used to meditate only for four or five minutes every day, but there was one thing, by His grace I remained absorbed all the while in the sacred thought of the Master. He is the only God to me. (p.337)

— ❖ —

Ajna is the distributor of power which we receive from above. Those who meditate on *ajna* feel the wavering condition and not the settled one. I have no experience of that sort of meditation but I think it to be so. Meditation on *sahasra* is better than that on *ajna*. Our last approach is when structure falls off and we feel ourself nowhere, while in the state of perfect Negation. An Urdu poet refers to the same condition in the following verse:

"*Ham wahan hain jahan se ham ko bhi kuch hamari khabar nahi ati*." (We are wherefrom we do not get any tidings of our own self even.) (p.344)

— ❖ —

At your present stage of progress it is not essential for an abhyasi to practise meditation, but since I want that the Central region may remain continually active for some time, I recommend meditation still, though as you have yourself written that the Central region is in action. (p.346)

Now for the sake of amusement I may relate a few funny incidents that have come to my knowledge. When Shri K. Swami occupied this house, the bug menace there was great that all drugs and medicines applied for the purpose failed to stop their heavy raids. For some time he was greatly worried not knowing what else to do. At last finding no other alternative he resorted to prayer and meditation. As a result today we find not a single bug troubling us here.

Another incident equally funny relates thus. Once he was staying with some of his friends in the same room. One of them, being in the habit of snoring heavily was a source of great trouble to all of them. Finding no other solution he again sat down for meditation. For a time the snoring increased abnormally but afterwards it subsided and he was quite calm for some time, during which time they all went into sound sleep. Anyhow there was the least disturbance that night and all of them had a good sleep. (p.356-357)

— ❖ —

I meditated on your form for about three or four days and I felt soothing. I tell you reason for doing so. The silent force was marking within you with enormous speed and I wanted to reduce it. Since I cannot catch the Divine Hand I took part in it with the result that the velocity decreased and the benefit remained the same. (p.361)

— ❖ —

A man asked me as to why I do not take *agya chakra* as the point of meditation. I replied that the power for *pinda pradesh* comes in it and it distributes to the lower region. If one meditates on this point he will feel something flickering disturbing the meditation. (p.386)

Letters of the Master, Volume II—1960 to 1971
[Letters by Babuji to Dr. K.C. Varadachari]

The case of Meher Baba is yet a mystery to me. I am of course definite that he has not attained liberation. I meditated on his early life and found the image of Lord Krishna in his heart then a form of some goddess appeared. ... I shall consider his case further for the sake of interest and give you my views, privately. But if you meditate on his mature age you will yourself come to the conclusion, as your super-conscious state of higher type has been awakened. (p.48-49)

— ❖ —

You have written to me that you are waiting for the reply to the questions. I do not know, is there any other letter containing the questions which might have been misplaced. You do not require any meditation but I am waiting the orders from my Master for it. Your *anubhav* about your condition that you feel absorbed in the centre with the calm feeling, is correct. I feel that you are being absorbed in it day by day. Your condition is really inexpressible because the words are wanting. When I meditate on your condition I feel that the refined or pure grace of God is pouring on you or in other words you are inhaling what is there in a way that your system is being divinised. (p.74)

— ❖ —

Now you complain about the encroachment of thoughts during meditation, for that I would earnestly say that during transmission, as my Master says in one of his writings, that the *sookshma sharir* of the teacher enters the body of the abhyasis knowingly or unknowingly, which brings the wavy thoughts which the abhyasis have. Of course, they may be translated in a way that you think them as yours. Happily you have got very good abhyasis, so the bad and vicious thoughts get no chance to attack you. I unfortunately found a few men whom when I transmitted, I was feeling the squalid sensation within me. I then refused to accept them as members of the Mission. There is one case in which I found when I transmitted to him that the pictures of naked fair sex were coming to me as he was a perfect debauch. So I did not take him into the Mission. My Master too had met with similar observations in two cases. If you want to minimize such thoughts occurring in you, you may give suggestions to your individual mind to stop such working during transmission and it will be helpful. But this process should not be done very frequently because you know many things of the abhyasis by the help of the individual mind. (p.81-82)

— ❖ —

I think you remember that I wrote to you some time ago that you do not require any meditation now, though then I was waiting for my Master's orders in this connection. Now my Master also is of the same opinion and says that you need not meditate as you used to do, but devote that part of the time also to the work of the Mission. (p.115)

— ❖ —

I am very happy to learn that regularly you do the meditation. If it is aided by 'transmission' it brings easy success. If you so desire to utilize my humble services towards the divine pursuit, I shall be able to do it from this place—the distance is no bar to transmission. [Letter to Robert Koch of Germany] (p.124-125)

— ❖ —

You have requested me to have awareness of your condition. Please meditate going at the depth of your condition to know what you are this day. Do you feel any sort of satisfaction in the heart? What is the condition of your thoughts? Are they minimized? Really speaking I do not know myself if I am aware of my condition, although there is no restlessness; and contentment and satisfaction are there. (p.145)

You may not for the present transmit to abhyasis till your headache is completely cured. I do not mean of course to forbid you for it but only for the purpose of avoiding strain lest it might aggravate your trouble. Satsanghis can however sit for group meditation in your room and they will experience as good a condition as they do when you transmit. (p.187)

— ❖ —

If you meditate that you are being cured of diabetes you will feel that it is gone. (p.189)

— ❖ —

I wrote to you that you can get rid of diabetes by meditation. The process is the same what we do in our daily meditation. Disease is going out of the body in the form of vapour or smoke and auto-suggestions to cure the disease. Of course, there are some other methods also for instance drawing energy from *brahmanda mandal* for the sun to cure the disease. You wrote to me that you have been feeling that you are absolutely doing nothing at all. It reminded me of *nishkam karma* given in Gita. This is the stage where this thing is possible. You do not require any meditation now; that has been withdrawn already (vide my previous letters) so you should spend that time in some other work of the Mission (Master's words in the same letter). (p.193)

— ❖ —

If anybody tries to meditate upon the Centre, his efforts will not be successful, though in his imagination he may however take the Centre in view to meditate upon. The only way for that would be the one I have hinted at in *Anant-Ki-Or* [*Towards Infinity*], but I forbid you and every body to attempt it. I had attempted it twice (with prayers to the Master) only for two or three seconds each time, because of the immense power there on the border ring. I had myself put a strong check over my heart and at the same time the Master's powerful hand was also there. Even then I could only peep into it but not meditate upon, at all, because the pressure on the heart was unbearably great. Moreover, it is very difficult even to approach the ring because of a strong backward push from it. The Master had however admonished me for it and warned me against repetition. (p.257-258)

— ❖ —

You say you have no peace... etc. This is obviously in contradiction with your previous statements even at lower stages of advancement. That means your advance has carried you farther away from peace, hence no advancement in the true sense. But this is very surprising since you acknowledge that your associates are getting peace and calmness through you in spite of your irritability. You have tried to reconcile the two views on the basis of my theory of parallelism. But then you seem to be ignoring your part of the work (getting humanity merged in the Divine).

The root cause of all this, in my opinion, is the uncalled for brooding over sorrowful reflections, taking into view their darker aspect. This indirectly amounts to meditation on miseries and sorrows. Hence the inevitable result must naturally be the growth of adverse effect. This we have therefore to be very particular about and try to avoid at all cost. But how can that be done? It can be only through resignation, dedication and submission to His will. Prayer does not imply dictation or enforcement of our will upon God, but submission to his will, laying down our sorrows and ills before Him. (p.274)

India in the West

Shri P. Rajagopalachari

"What is the use in knowing myself? I know what I am, but what I have to know is what I must be or ought to be. That is the purpose of life. Some people have taught meditation on this idea too, of knowing the self. But suppose you meditate on the idea 'who am I'—well, the concentration is only on the 'I', so that egoism will grow. Look here, we meditate and egoism grows! So what is the use of this meditation? It is my view that we must forget ourselves and then only we can find Him. I may be wrong but this is my view. Now people have craving for God. It is everywhere, but people do not develop spirituality. Why? Because they do not know how to approach Him." [Babuji]

(p.69-70)

— ❖ —

After the meditation sitting we sat out in the garden—it was sunny and pleasant, though surprisingly, Master felt a little cold. Some people asked questions which Master personally answered.

Q: Why should we meditate on the heart? For me I find it is better if I meditate on the head.

Master [Babuji]: This is **the** method. For us it is the **only** method.

Q: I have been doing mantra meditation. Is it better or is your method better?

Master: It all depends on your experience. If you find you are improving in your method then continue it. If not, search for another method. (p.71)

— ❖ —

Q: I was told that when you are trying to receive this transmission you have to meditate on the heart. Is that right?

PR: Yes, we meditate on light in the heart. My Master says that the heart is the most suitable for meditation because it is the heart that is the seat of life. It is also the seat of emotion. And, traditionally in all religions, God is supposed to be seated in the heart. There are other points for meditation but my Master says they have only limited effect, mainly physical, as against the total **spiritual** effect of human transformation that we seek in our Sahaj Marg yoga.

Q: But isn't the point between the eyes more suitable?

PR: Well, it is certainly more popular and well known because even in the Bhagavad Gita that point is mentioned—*the ajna chakra*. But according to my Master the *ajna chakra* is the point of distribution of power to the human system. So by meditating on that point we may acquire power, but not spiritual growth. There is also another interpretation, that the *ajna chakra* is a point suited to, and meant for, the *sannyasi*, the ascetics who renounce life, but it is not suited for the house-holder. (p.90-91)

— ❖ —

Q: Why do some people not get the deep feeling of peace in meditation?

Master: Because even though they are doing meditation properly, they are behind *Being*. (p.124)

— ❖ —

Q: Meditation is passive. You do nothing. How can it give results?

Master: We meditate on the heart supposing Divine light to be there. It means you are playing on your own heart, which is itself a sport and a work. You know you are meditating, that means doing something; and the place on which you work, the heart, is also there. And you have to reach your goal; this idea is also there, and you wait for something subconsciously. That means you are not inert but so busy that you are doing three things at the same time. So passivity is lost in activity! (p.142)

— ❖ —

Q: What is the power of mantras?

Master: In Sahaj Marg we do not advocate mantra recitation.

Q: But do they have any power?

Master: Well, it is said mantras have power because many people have taught this. But in my opinion, meditation alone can lead to the real goal. (p.151)

— ❖ —

In the course of after-dinner talks with Master the talk turned towards visions and experiences in meditation. Master explained that visions are unnecessary and have, really speaking, no value as indicators of spiritual progress. A vision is nothing but a locked-up impression being allowed to surface by the cleaning process. Therefore, all that come out as visions are nothing but earlier impressions formed in us by our own thoughts and actions. (p.156)

— ❖ —

The third lesson that emerges is this extreme and fundamental humility that we must strive to develop in ourselves. This can come only by ridding ourselves of our individual ego by constant meditation and constant remembrance, and by striving to develop in our sadhana to achieve a final stage of total surrender and submission to the Master. (p.234)

My Master

Shri P. Rajagopalachari

All yogic teachers have advised their students to set apart a room specially for their prayers and meditation. The idea behind this of course is to have a room where the atmosphere is kept pure, uncontaminated by normal life routines. Master's teaching expands this to the ultimate dimension of a pure and holy universe, where the whole universe becomes a prayer room. The older idea is restrictive. It seeks to enclose purity into a small place, implying that the rest of the home may be impure. Master says this is not sufficient. We may begin at one point, our own hearts, but the seed of purity sown there must be nurtured and made to grow in such a manner that it radiates beyond the confines of the individual human system, radiates beyond his home and beyond his small world until, finally, the whole universe comes within its divine embrace. (p.24)

— ❖ —

Master has stated that most humans start life as animals, and to humanize them becomes the first step in sadhana. The animal man becomes a real human by the practice of meditation which regulates mental functions, and thereby makes it possible for the regulation to percolate down to the physical level. It is with the mind that we have to begin. Any process which starts with the body is then obviously putting the cart before the horse. Meditation is the abhyasi's part, the part he has to play in this divine adventure. The Master's work is to clean the abhyasi of past samskaras and to transmit to him. (p.26)

— ❖ —

"I have said prayer is begging but meditation is receiving. Why? Because when we sit for meditation we sit in a receptive attitude so that a vacuum is created in the heart. Only an empty vessel can be filled! Who can fill a vessel that is already full? You see the difference? They beg [laughing], while we receive! This is the greatness of our system. It is Lalaji's grace that such a simple system of greatest efficacy is available to us today. But few take advantage of it. What to say, many people even say they have no time! I prescribed one hour for the morning meditation originally. Now I have reduced it to half an hour. Even this people are not willing to do.

I will tell you an enjoyable story. A person once came to me. He was a big officer of the government at Delhi. He came to me with one of our associates. He wanted to know something about our system and so I told him. When he heard that he had to meditate for half an hour he said it was impossible, as he was too busy to spare so much time. So I asked him to reduce it. He again said he was too busy. I then told him to do ten minutes a day. Look here! He got angry. He said, 'What is this *tamasha*! I am telling you I am a very busy man and you are going on asking me to do it. I cannot spare even five minutes a day.' Now Lalaji gave me an idea. Look how he helps us! I asked this officer, 'Can you tell me whether there is anybody more busy than you?' He got angry again. He said, 'What a foolish question this is? Of course there are people more busy than I am. The Prime Minister is much more busy than I am!' I then told him not to take an extreme example but to think of someone just a little more busy than him. He said his neighbour was a bigger officer and more busy than himself. So you know what I told him? [exploding into laughter] I told him 'Saheb, give me the difference between your busyness and his busyness. That will give some time for meditation.' Poor man, he thought I was making fun of him and went away quite annoyed." [Babuji]

Master then told me another instance of like nature when a person claimed he was too busy to meditate. Master said, "You know what I told him? I told him God is to be blamed for not creating the day with more than twenty-four hours in it. It is God's fault. If he had created the day with twenty-six hours such busy persons would have had time for meditation." [Babuji]

(p.98-99)

— ❖ —

To illustrate this first stage of Master's work I would like to relate the case of a person who is now a senior preceptor of the Mission. It was about fifteen years ago that this gentleman read a review of Master's *Reality at Dawn* in the newspapers. He wrote to Master, evincing interest in the Sahaj Marg method of yogic training offered by the book. Master replied that his services were at the disposal of this gentleman, and requested him to give the method a trial by sitting in meditation. Master requested this gentleman to give him prior information as to when he wanted to sit in meditation so that he could transmit at the appropriate time. Relating this story this gentleman told me, "When I got Master's letter I decided that while I would sit in meditation I would not give him prior information about it. After all he claimed to be able to impart the training by transmission. So why should I tell him in advance? In a sense I wanted to test him. Thinking like this I sat down to meditate the very next morning. It was a most wonderful experience. Within moments of my sitting I felt a tremendous power flowing into my heart. It was as if molten lead was being poured into me." This gentleman realised that Master was not dependent on his information to commence his work. His divine work had commenced much earlier. It was only necessary for the abhyasi to feel it by an act of conscious participation in the work. (p.128-129)

— ❖ —

As this cleaning proceeds the abhyasi experiences actual 'lightness' during his meditation sittings.

I had a personal problem in this connection which I once discussed with Master. When I first started meditation a great number of thoughts used to come up and intrude but, on following Master's technique of not attending to thoughts, the inrush of thoughts became progressively reduced until I could experience intervals of thoughtlessness. But, and this was my problem, after a few years of *sadhana* I suddenly found thoughts of a most sordid and vile nature coming during meditation. Naturally I was considerably perturbed because I was apprehensive that this might indicate not progress but regress. Master quickly cleared the problem up for me. He said, "You see, the dust that settles every day on the table can be easily dusted off. It is superficial and easy to remove. Suppose ink has been poured on the table and allowed to soak, then the cleaning is more difficult. So the nature of the impression makes the difference. Now I tell you one more thing. We sometimes have bad thoughts, I mean consciously. We feel ashamed and push them down. Now the very bad or worst thoughts are hidden away deep inside the mind. So in cleaning they may come up last of all. In your case this is what has happened. You should be happy that these vile thoughts have been removed at last." (p.133)

— ❖ —

"When we sit in meditation there is a craving in the heart for something. This creates a vacuum, and grossness from the surrounding atmosphere is attracted and becomes deposited on us. A person who is meditating properly therefore accumulates some grossness like this also." [Babuji] (p.134)

— ❖ —

"At death the mind should be made a complete blank. No thoughts must be allowed to come into it, not even of gods or anything like that. It must be made completely blank so that at death it can merge with the source where the condition is that of nothingness. And I tell you, for the abhyasis of our *sanstha* this is very easy because this is what they are taught to do every time they sit in meditation. To us this becomes second nature. When we sit in meditation the mind becomes thoughtless, and so what we are experiencing, to put it in one way, is a condition somewhat like that at death. You may call it a condition of death-in-life if you like. So when the time comes we automatically get into this state of mind, and there is no impediment even at the last moment." [Babuji] (p.138-139)

— ❖ —

Speaking in a very general manner, experiences can be classified as falling into three groups. The first group contains experiences arising out of the abhyasi's own imagination, or as a result of his having projected them himself. Abhyasis, indeed all human beings, are prone to discuss matters among themselves, and to exchange notes on each other's experiences. In spiritual *sadhana* this is not advisable since, in the same sitting, different abhyasis may undergo different experiences. This does not mean that one is progressing more, or faster, than another. Experiences depend on such diverse factors as the *samskaras* of the individual, his previous background, social environment and so on. If abhyasis discuss each other's experience, some may feel that they are not getting the right experience from meditation, and may feel dejected. Worse, they may project the same things unconsciously during subsequent sittings and have experiences which are their own creation. Therefore, Master advises abhyasis not to discuss their spiritual experiences with each other, but only with Master himself or with the preceptor. Such experiences are not true spiritual experiences and have no value whatsoever.

The second group covers all experiences arising from the cleaning process. Master has stated that when the system of the abhyasi is cleaned, then the past impressions are removed. When these impressions surface to the mind then the original experience or activity which created the impressions is once again created in the mind. So the abhyasi has an 'experience'. In general the experiences which abhyasis have are of this category. The visions of gods and goddesses that abhyasis experience during meditation are of this type. Whenever such an experience comes up, it is an indication of a past involvement with that particular deity. I have referred elsewhere to one such experience where Master himself saw a monkey in the place of an abhyasi. Many abhyasis have startlingly clear visions of gods or saints. Quite a few make the tragic mistake of thinking that the goal has been reached, since their chosen personal god has granted them his *darshan*. It is a pity that persons who practise without the guidance of a capable Master mistake such experiences for divine revelations, and go back to the traditional forms of worship of that particular deity which appeared to them. Abhyasis have to be on their guard against such misinterpretation of experiences. Many abhyasis report having visions of gardens, hill-stations and the like. These also belong to the same category. Some experiences may also refer to a previous life. Generally the abhyasi will not be able to know this. But Master and the preceptors will be able to correctly interpret and evaluate such experiences, particularly if they have occurred during sittings with the Master or the preceptor.

The third category contains what Master has referred to as 'revelatory experiences'. These are of a very valuable nature as they contain messages from the inner Self of the abhyasi which, if properly interpreted, can help him considerably on his journey. Such experiences may come during meditation sittings, or as dreams. Master has also stated that orders, instructions, and advice from the Master himself can be conveyed in this way.

(p.146-149)

— ❖ —

During this second sleep I had a dream. ... Lalaji spoke to me. He said, "So far you have been meditating in one way. I shall now teach you another method. Meditate on my form as that from which the entire manifested universe has been created." Though Lalaji spoke, the voice I heard was that of my Master Babuji Maharaj. As soon as I woke up I sat in meditation, meditating as advised for over an hour. The meditation was very deep and I was in a condition like that of *samadhi*. My depression vanished. It was as if a new beginning was made. When I reported this experience to Master he exclaimed, "You have had a wonderful experience. A secret has been revealed to you. You know what it is? It has been revealed to you that my Master and I are one, though people see us as separate beings." (p.150)

— ❖ —

One morning Master gave me an individual sitting. I felt deeply absorbed, and lost to this world. Towards the end of the sitting, for a few minutes, I suddenly felt myself floating in an ocean of brilliance. Brilliance is perhaps not the right description. Luminescence would be more apt. All around me was nothing but sky—nothing but sky above me, below me and all around me. Perhaps I should call it space instead of sky. I was seated in the usual meditation posture, and I was floating serenely in that space which was a luminous soft blue in appearance. There was no one else, nothing else, in the whole universe but me. Not even Master! It was an ecstatic experience. Even when I became momentarily conscious during meditation the impression persisted that I was alone, absolutely and blissfully alone, in the whole immensity of space! After the sitting Master asked me how I felt. I described my experience to him. Master said, "You have been given a taste of Eternity. This generally comes at higher levels but you have been given it today."

I asked Master how this state could be made permanent, my own as it were. Master laughed and said, "*Puja* is the only method. I mean meditation, as we are taught to do it. But I tell you one thing. In *puja* the head must bend in submission. If you are conscious that you are doing *puja* then that is not *puja*. I will tell you another thing. In *puja* we go to God to receive His grace. God has everything. After all He is God! So He has everything. But what happens when we go to Him? We go with small bags. What can He fill inside such a small bag? Therefore we must become deserving vessels for His grace. This is essential. And this is what we do by our practice of meditation and cleaning. We are transformed into vessels fit to receive His grace when He wishes to pour it into us." (p.157-158)

— ❖ —

"Meditation is the only way. But it must be correctly done. Meditation really means that the mind may be accustomed to the Centre itself, instead of working elsewhere. At the human level the mind is wandering hither and thither, dragging us with it. It takes work from us! But by meditation we regulate it, and start taking work from it. I tell you an important thing. The mind is the instrument of realisation. It is also the instrument of our downfall." [Babuji] (p.159-160)

"Then Lalaji answered, 'See, realisation is such a condition which we may perhaps think of as valueless, but without it our very existence is impossible.' But," added Master, "I am not prepared to reveal its secret yet. But one thing I will tell you. If realisation can be explained it will no longer be realisation. If God can be explained or defined He ceases to be God. Both these things can't be limited. I am giving you this hint! I will tell you one more thing. When a person has attained the state of realisation then self is gone. At that stage if you try to meditate, the self will not come to your mind at all." (p.163)

Sahaj Marg in Europe

Shri P. Rajagopalachari

Q: I mean, how much time is needed for meditation?

Master: You can start from twenty minutes and take it up to one hour. (p.10)

— ❖ —

PR: ...When we start meditation we start thinking of somebody other than ourselves. So the attention is transferred from the self to something else. ...

Now what happens in meditation is that Master gives you an object for meditation, which is light in the heart. And light as the object of our meditation was not accidental, because even though we ultimately try to reach something which is abstract, without qualities, without form, without name, very few people can really meditate on the abstract. For instance, if I say I will give you zero Rupees or zero Marks it makes no sense; but without zero you would have no mathematics. Similarly, Master has given us an object of meditation which has no form, which cannot be described. Light cannot be described. You can only say light is light. Master has said that it is the only object which is an object and yet almost abstract. Now when we meditate on such an object no doubt the mind is put on that, but the mind cannot desire or want to possess it. It is an object which we can love but which we cannot possess. We need light but we never possess light. So the mind becomes trained to forget the self, and to move towards something else which is yet so abstract that we cannot want it, or desire it or possess it. So, in this way, when we train the mind or regulate the mind, naturally and systematically during meditation, no impressions are formed. (p.81-84)

— ❖ —

PR: ...By meditation we start in the morning, we think of the Master; in the evening we meditate, we think of the Master; at bedtime we meditate, we again think of the Master. This is at least a minimum of three times we think of him, if we do the practice as specified. (p.86)

Blossoms in the East
Shri P. Rajagopalachari

Q: Why cannot we meditate on any object of our choice? The ancient texts specify so many things, including the sky, the sea, etc. I would prefer to meditate on the sea. To me it gives a true idea of infinity. Can I do so?

Master: Well, it is for you to decide. In the system developed by my Master, we meditate on light in the heart. It is a mere supposition.

Q: But can I meditate on the sea?

Master: Well. My idea is that if you meditate upon something, you must get the essence of it as the result. So if you meditate on the sea, you will get salt! [laughter] (p.109)

The Garden of Hearts

Shri P. Rajagopalachari

...Master told us of an abhyasi who came to him and said he wanted to give up meditation. Master asked him why he wanted to stop it. The abhyasi replied that he found that during meditation the breathing slowed down considerably. This lead to reduced intake of oxygen and the abhyasi felt that if the oxygen intake became so reduced, it might reduce his longevity. Master said, "Look here. His feeling was correct. The breathing becomes very slow during meditation. His complaint was therefore genuine. I examined my own condition during meditation and found that the breathing stopped completely for several minutes at a time. This was my own experience. Then I came to the conclusion that there must be an organ in the body itself which produces oxygen inside. I do not know if I am right in this." After saying this Master became silent. After sitting quietly for a few minutes he looked at us and said, "Yes! There is an organ or something like that in the body which produces oxygen inside. Now I have confirmation for it. I have just received the confirmation." Karl Gutsche was deeply interested in this. He asked Master how to locate the organ. Master smilingly answered, "That is your work. It is for scientists like you to do research and find it out!" Master then said, "It is my finding that meditation actually increases the span of human life." (p.66-67)

— ❖ —

Q (Dave Bolevice): As an abhyasi continues to meditate year after year will the process become easier or will thoughts continue to come?

Master: The intensity of the thoughts will be reduced, but not in a day. Meditate longer and bring it up to one hour. Then see the results.

Dave: It is very difficult.

Master: Only because you are not doing it. I can easily do it. I am not a special person, and if I can do it you can also do it.

(p.78)

— ❖ —

PR: ...In Sahaj Marg we have a state or condition called *sahaj samadhi*. It is a condition in which an abhyasi is totally absorbed **inside**, and yet alert and aware of the outside. It is called *sahaj samadhi*. It is a natural state which is supposed to be the God-like state. It is a condition of total absorption coupled with total awareness. You will have noticed in our system of meditation that even when you are in the deepest state of meditation, deeply absorbed inside, when Master says, "That is all," you are immediately aware of it. If it was the other traditional type of *samadhi*, you would have to be forcibly awakened out of it. (p.102)

— ❖ —

Q: How to imagine the light in the heart? Is it necessary?

PR: It is necessary.

Q: Master has said that abhyasis can meditate on His form.

PR: That is only for abhyasis who have become so devoted to him that he is the light in their hearts.

Q: When, during meditation, we are disturbed by our thoughts, etc., how are we to go back to the meditation on the light in the heart?

PR: There is only one way. When you know that the thought has gone away from that of the light in the heart to something else, bring it back to the thought of the light in the heart. Do this without force. Master says we must ignore the other thoughts. I would request H to explain that when thoughts disturb us during meditation, it is our attention to such thoughts that gives them the power to disturb us. They have no power of their own. So, if they are ignored, they drop off by themselves. Master has said that we must treat such thoughts very much like uninvited guests. Don't pay them any attention; they will themselves go away. (p.105-106)

— ❖ —

PR: Now when a person comes and says that he has been doing Sahaj Marg meditation for three years, and adds that his problems have increased instead of decreasing, that shows a wrong understanding of Sahaj Marg. If you know that all these problems arise because of samskaras, and the sufferings or **experiences** arise because of what we call as the *bhoga* of samskara, then you will not give so much importance to what you are experiencing. It is all quickly washed out. Now if you think over what you are feeling again and again; for instance if you go on thinking, "I am in pain. Oh! I am in pain," that becomes a meditation in itself, as I told you a couple of days ago, on pain, and therefore it increases the suffering, reinforces the pain, instead of decreasing or reducing it. (p.135)

— ❖ —

Q: Why, when I am sitting in meditation, do I become warm?

PR: Sometimes you may also feel cold. It does not matter. Sometimes it may be purely physical. You should write it in the diary and then forget it.

Q: When we are gathered with the Master and together all day, is it advisable to do one's own practice, for instance meditation if it is morning, or cleaning if it is in the evening?

PR: You always meditate in the morning according to the system prescribed by the Master. If you are having the evening sitting here, then there is no need to separately do the cleaning. The night prayer meditation should be done by you before you go to bed. (p.138)

— ❖ —

Tony Bernardi: When a preceptor is sick, seriously sick, with high fever or something like that, and someone comes to him, can he give him a sitting?

PR: No. I request all of you to consider extending this principle also to the Master. When the Master is unwell, when he is resting, we should not pester him for sittings or for interviews. And, most importantly, we should not sit in meditation in his presence without his knowledge and permission. (p.184)

Proceedings of the Seminar on Sahaj Marg

Held at Vorauf—Munich, Germany,
April 27th to May 4th, 1985
Shri P. Rajagopalachari

Meditation means to think continuously about one thing, and we are supposed to take as the object of meditation that which we wish to achieve. And here, because we are involved in realisation, God realisation, Self realisation, therefore the object has to be of that Nature. The goal of Sahaj Marg is an abstract goal called the Ultimate Self. Therefore we cannot have any name or form for meditation. Nor can we have even any qualities or attributes of Divinity. However, Master felt that for most people it would be impossible to meditate on the abstract. So, in Sahaj Marg, our Master has taken as the object of meditation what he thought, what he knows, what he has experienced to be the subtlest thing that we can have for meditation without making it gross or with a form or with a name, and that is: Divine light in the heart. So this has to be very clearly understood that in Sahaj Marg, the object of meditation is Divine light in the heart and nothing else.

And as I already told you, meditation means to think continuously of the same thing. What we do is to sit comfortably with our eyes closed, and have the thought that our heart is filled with Divine light. We sit comfortably because during the period of meditation the body should not interfere, and break our meditation. In the Sahaj Marg system there is no special *asana* prescribed. Patanjali himself described *asana* as something which you can hold comfortably over a period of time. So we are allowed to choose a position in which we can comfortably sit for one hour. But we are not allowed to lie down and meditate; because if we lie down and meditate, the relaxation produced will put us to sleep. During meditation, if we have to change our position it is permitted, because the object is to be in such a situation that the body does not disturb.

Regarding the light in the heart, we are not supposed to see it or try to see any light in the heart. As Babuji Maharaj has explained, it is a mere supposition that the light is there. Now we are supposed to have this idea, or the thought, continuously for one hour. The prescribed period is one hour and not less. Nor are we supposed to meditate for more than an hour at one time. But if we have spare time, there is no harm in breaking the meditation, relaxing for ten minutes and then meditating for another hour again. After the first hour... you may break it for some time.

When we sit for meditation, we will of course have disturbing thoughts. We are taught not to attend to thoughts but to ignore them. Because Master's research shows that when we attend to those thoughts, the thought takes power from us, and becomes stronger and stronger. So, when we ignore the thought we find it drops off! There may be another thought in its place, but it is treated in the same way. Master says: "Treat them as uninvited guests and they will go away." If we do this systematically and with alertness we will find that in hardly a few months we can reach a state of thoughtlessness.

Here, it is necessary to understand that all these thoughts come from inside us, our own thoughts in the form of samskaras. If we attend to the thoughts when they rise, they become powerful, they multiply and they go back inside. But when we are not attending to them, we allow them to fall off, the inner store of samskara becomes exhausted quickly, that is how we reach a state of thoughtlessness during meditation. It is of course necessary to remember that thoughtlessness is not our goal.

So I think that I have dealt with the morning meditation, except to say that it should be done before sunrise as Babuji has instructed. Master has clarified that at the time when the night meets the day and the day meets the night, there is a balance in nature. And when we meditate at that point of balance in nature, it helps us very much in our progress to achieve quickly our goal. Of course, this applies to normal situations when there is a day and a night! Please don't ask me what we should do at the North Pole or the South Pole! But wherever and whenever possible, this is how it should be done. (p.34-36)

— ❖ —

The greatest benefit of the meditation in the morning is that it trains us to regulate our minds. As Babuji Maharaj put it, instead of our being the slaves of our mind, we have to become the Masters of our minds. So, by holding one thought in the mind during meditation, we slowly gain, progressively, more and more ability to regulate that mind. We use the mind to regulate the mind. (p.40)

— ❖ —

So meditation helps us to regulate the mind, and by regulating it ninety-five percent of our problems are solved. Meditation is therefore a process, not a goal in itself. But it is a process which helps us immensely and therefore we do it. (p.41)

— ❖ —

"We have lost our naturalness, which we have to restore, and it is the Sahaj Marg system, which can restore in us the original condition. Meditation is something waiting for our originality, and transmission is the central force which is giving that thing." [Babuji] (p.78)

The Principles of Sahaj Marg, Volume I
Shri P. Rajagopalachari

In raja yoga the main method of development is the art of meditation. Meditation may be defined as the continuous thinking of something, or about something. In a sense, therefore, anybody who is thinking continuously of something may be said to be involved in meditation. Ancient teachers, both in the East and the West, have taught that as one meditates so one becomes. It therefore follows that what we meditate upon we get or become and, inversing this formula, if we want to become something we must meditate upon **that** and nothing else. Therefore, if our aim is Realisation or the attainment of one-ness with the Ultimate, the object of meditation must be that Ultimate, and nothing else. Raja yoga, in its purest form, excludes physical objects of meditation including the figures or forms of the various gods and goddesses of the Hindu pantheon. The object of meditation must be limited to the formless, attributeless, abstract Ultimate.

In Sahaj Marg, which my Master has developed as a purified form of raja yoga, and which system was re-discovered by his Master, Samartha Guru Shri Ram Chandraji of Fatehgarh, the correct way of meditation with the implicit and specified goal of realisation is taught. In this system meditation is on this object, viz., the abstract ultimate alone, because meditation on lesser objects can only lead to lesser achievements or accomplishments, falling short of the established goal.

In the Sahaj Marg system the student is asked to meditate on the heart. Ancient yoga systems teach meditation on the point of the nose, on the point between the eyebrows, on a point in the forehead, and so on. My Master has excluded such points and prescribed it on the heart for three important reasons. Firstly, the heart is the seat of life, and therefore, when we meditate on this point we meditate on the source of life itself. Secondly, circulation commences from the heart and if the heart is purified, the purity extends throughout the human organization. Thirdly, all religions have stated and taught that in the human being it is in the heart that the Creator has his abode, and therefore this is the fitting point for meditation.

My Master recognizes that the abstract Ultimate as an object of meditation is a very difficult one for beginners. He, therefore, specifies light as the initial object, the method being to imagine that the heart is illuminated from inside by the presence of the Divine who resides therein. I must stress that this is only the beginning, and in fact we are advised not to meditate on light as a source of light, which should lead to wrong results. It is like the diving board in a swimming pool where the board enables the diver to get sufficient momentum to take off, and after the diver has taken off, the board has no further use for him until he dives again.

In our Sahaj Marg system all that you are asked to do is to sit comfortably, close your eyes, and do this meditation. My Master states that as one progresses in meditation the body acquires for itself a posture of repose and tranquillity which it can hold for the length of time necessary, and therefore, *asana* becomes established in a natural manner. Similarly as meditation progresses our experience testifies to the fact that breathing slows down and assumes a natural cycle, natural to that state of existence, and so *pranayama* becomes established. Under my Master's direction as the pupil progresses in meditation, purification of the heart proceeds automatically, and mental processes are purified which in turn results in pure action, and therefore *yama* and *niyama*, the first two stages of Patanjali's yoga also become naturally established. As yet another result of meditation, the mind becomes used to thinking about one fixed thing, and as the mind's capacity grows, the power of concentration becomes established and this capacity grows so that it results finally in a stage where concentration becomes natural, and thus *pratyahara* and *dharana* aspects of yoga also become established. Thus by commencing at the seventh stage of Patanjali's

Ashtanga Yoga under the guidance of an able Master the earlier six stages become naturally established without any undue physical or mental effort on the part of the practicant being necessary. (p.18-21)

— ❖ —

Now we teach, or at least our religion teaches, that by being trained to worship God outside us and reaching perfection in that form of worship, we must then advance to the next stage which we call spirituality, where we start worshipping God inside us, the immanent deity. This is mysticism, which we call yoga in the East. Therefore, a transfer of worship of the deity from outside ourselves to inside our own heart, and seeking communion with Him within ourselves is what mysticism or yoga really means. This is what my Master is trying to teach. The only way possible to achieve this communion is meditation.

...we should try to follow this mystic path and seek the deity within ourselves, and the way, as I have already stated, is meditation. That is, by closing our eyes and sitting comfortably and in a sense if I may say so, of relaxation, we put our thought on the Ultimate within ourselves and try to commune with Him by constant thought of Him. Meditation literally means to think continuously of one thing, or to hold one thought continuously in the mind. This is meditation. What my Master teaches is precisely this, and we call it raja yoga in India meaning the king of all yogas.

By practising this yoga we are able to slowly strengthen our association with the deity by constantly meditating on His presence inside our heart in the form of illumination. This is our system of yoga which we call Sahaj Marg or the natural way of realisation. We sit in a detached or a relaxed way, comfortably, and have the thought or try to hold in our mind this thought that the heart is illuminated from within by the presence of the spark of the Ultimate deity that is present within us. This, in brief, is what my Master teaches and I hope it will be possible for you all to practise this and derive such benefit as exists in it. (p.30-31)

The rishis of the ancient times used to sit in meditation continuously for days, weeks and, if legends be true, months and years too, without a break. They had therefore neither the opportunity nor perhaps the inclination for physical exercise. However, the body had to have a minimum tension imposed on it to keep it fit at least to a minimal extent. Therefore, the rishis devised a system of yoga postures which they could adopt one after the other while sitting in meditation or contemplation, and thus kill two birds, as it were, with one stone.

Sahaj Marg yoga also does not recognize the need for the next two steps in Patanjali's yoga, but it really starts as the seventh stage, *dhyana*, or meditation leading to the final step or stage of mergence with the Ultimate. My Master's teaching indicates that when the highest activity is performed, i.e., when meditation is established, the body assumes the posture natural and convenient to it. Thus *asana* is established by itself, not in an artificial or contorted way, but according to the needs of the body of the individual. Similarly, when meditation is established the breathing slows down and assumes its own cycle, and *pranayama* is thus established. When the mind becomes purified by meditation, the first two steps of *yama* and *niyama* are also established naturally and automatically. A poor mind can think nothing but poor thoughts, and poor thoughts can lead to nothing but poor actions. But when the mind is purified and correctly directed, pure thoughts and pure actions result. Therefore, when we commence with meditation and establish it firmly, all the other steps of the yoga of Patanjali become automatically established in us. (p.43-44)

— ❖ —

But when the tendencies of the mind are slowly turned inwards, and the mind is itself attracted by what it finds inside, the outside world loses any charm that it has had up to now. And by the very loss of that, there is renunciation. That is, instead of our giving up the world, the world gives us up! Because now the mind is no longer externalized, it does not go out.

This then is what my Master teaches, first turn the mind inwards. Now what is the way to do this? Sit in meditation, because it is only in meditation that we turn the mind upon ourselves. When I say ourselves, I do not mean this self (the body) but the inner self. We do this in our system of Sahaj Marg which my Master has evolved as a very simplified technique of meditation. We do not meditate on the psychic points of the body, we meditate on the heart. He prescribes meditation on the heart. He says the heart is the seat of life. According to all religions it is in the heart that the Divine resides. And physiologically, it is from the heart that circulation flows and everything else happens. If this point, the most important point in the human system, can be enriched and purified, then it must permeate to the rest of the whole system without our having to bother with the other parts, like the head, the muscles, the feet and so on. It is a radiant flow from the centre outward, from the centre to the whole system... (p.60-61)

— ❖ —

So we asked Master what is needed, or what is the preparation needed for meditation? He said, "Sit and meditate, that is the only preparation." Meditation is a simple thing. It is something to do with the mind and does not need any violent exercise or preparation.

Unfortunately there are systems which teach that it is necessary to prepare the mind, when meditation alone can prepare the mind. It is meditation which prepares the mind... (p.62)

— ❖ —

As I told you, we meditate on the heart imagining that inside the heart, by the presence of the Divine, the Ultimate, the heart is illuminated. We try to hold this thought for about thirty minutes initially when we sit in meditation. We close our eyes and sit comfortably so that the body does not interfere with the mind, that is all that is required. According to Patanjali himself, *asana* is something which is steady and comfortable, "*sthiram sukham asanam,*" this is what Patanjali has written. So we sit comfortably as we normally sit, and allow the body to rest in itself so that the mind can act in its own way. Hold, or try to hold, this thought that there is illumination in the heart. If other thoughts come into the mind as they surely will—because they are welling up from inside ourselves, they are not something which are imposed from outside, they are our own thoughts seeking to come out now that the mind is pegged on to something else—we allow them to go by not attending to them, by ignoring them. It is one of my Master's important techniques that if you do not attend to thoughts they have no power. It is our attention which gives to thoughts the power they hold over us. So we, in meditation, do not attend to these thoughts, we allow them to drop off by themselves. This is the technique of meditation that we are required to practise. (p.63-64)

— ❖ —

What he needs most is not our wealth or our physical energy or anything like that but a simple measure of co-operation, that we sit in meditation for the prescribed period and **allow** him to work on us with his transmission. (p.67-68)

— ❖ —

We are taught that we should sit in meditation for about an hour in the morning. Nowadays, Master specifies half an hour, but originally it used to be one hour. And about this meditation, we are often asked a question, "We are not able to concentrate. What should we do?" My Master has clarified that meditation is the process and the result is concentration. Now this concentration, by itself, is not of much value in our development because concentration is only the use of a power, and power, by itself, does not lead to evolution. But it has a positive advantage in our daily life because by meditation, when we are able to make the mind concentrate, we are able to exclude thoughts we don't require, or we don't wish to receive. Here I come to one of the most important teachings of my Master. When we have thoughts it is our attention, it is the power of our attention, that gives the power to the thought. A thought by itself has no power. It is the attention that we give it that gives the thought its power. By meditation if we are able to exclude such thoughts without fighting with them, without attending to them, then the mind achieves a state, a state of existence, a state of being, where a single thought alone can exist at a time. Thus the process of meditation gives us the ability to concentrate, or makes the mind come into a state of concentration, which we in India call one-pointedness.

Meditation must always have a purpose because nothing is purposeless. Even without bringing yoga into the picture, we are almost always meditating on something or the other. When we are looking for a higher standard of living, or when we are keenly pursuing a better job, we are constantly thinking of it. I say this because the correct definition of meditation is to think constantly of something. When we bring yoga into the picture we get confused as to what meditation really means. The only sense in which yogic meditation differs from our normal meditation is in the aim of that meditation, the purpose of that meditation. Therefore we have to meditate with a purpose in mind, and when we come into the field of yoga that purpose is evolution, or the fulfillment of human life to its highest perfect condition.

(p.73-75)

— ❖ —

Now coming to the practice itself, we are advised to sit in meditation three times a day, morning, evening and bedtime. What we do is to sit comfortably without any botheration about *asanas* or things like that. I mention this point particularly, because people think that without adopting an *asana*, meditation cannot be done. Patanjali, the codifier of yogic systems, has himself said that any position which can be held comfortably for a length of time is an *asana*. Therefore, it is not very important how we sit, or in what position we sit, so long as we can sit in that position for the length of time specified for our meditation. The only necessity is that the body should not disturb us during that period. So, having assumed a comfortable position, we close our eyes. Sometimes people ask us, "Can we meditate with eyes open?" It is certainly possible when we reach higher levels of spirituality, but not at the earlier stages. It is the eye which receives most of the impressions from the external world. Obviously it is better not to receive further impressions, because we are trying to remove the old impressions. Therefore we meditate with eyes closed.

In this particular system the meditation process is very specific because we have a specific aim, which is somewhat higher than what is normally specified in the West for yogic systems. As I said earlier, our purpose is to achieve the highest human possibilities. Now we meditate on the heart. What we meditate on is the heart. There are systems which meditate on other points, like the point between the eyebrows, the point of the nose, etc., but we meditate specifically on the heart for three very valid reasons, very important reasons.

The first point is that it is the heart which is the seat of life. The second point is that when we meditate on the heart the effect of that meditation spreads throughout the system. The third point is the most important, but often the least acceptable, and that is that the heart is the particular seat of whatever Divinity we possess.

Therefore, for these three important points or reasons, my Master specifies meditation on the heart. In the Sahaj Marg practice we meditate on the heart, imagining that there is effulgence or light in the heart. We don't try to see light or to project any light. We begin with the idea that there is light in the heart, and if there are disturbing thoughts, as I told you earlier, we just ignore them, because it is our own attention which gives power to them to disturb us. (p.76-77)

What the aspirant is taught to do is to sit in meditation in the morning at a suitable time, seated in a convenient posture. The process is to be repeated once again at bedtime and, in between, Master prescribes a cleaning process in which the aspirant has to clean out the daily accumulation of impressions which in Sanskrit we call *samskara*. In meditation the practicant is asked to imagine divine light pervading his heart and to meditate on that. Meditation is a process of continuously thinking about a single idea and does not mean concentration which, my Master teaches, is the result of meditation. If during the process of meditation other thoughts interrupt or flow into the mind, we are advised to gently ignore those thoughts and become inattentive to them. ... If this technique is meticulously followed, the aspirant will soon find himself arriving at periods of thoughtlessness during meditation, the thoughtlessness having been achieved almost effortlessly. It is important to remember during meditation that the process is entered into for the purpose of realising one's goal. This makes the process highly dynamic. (p.90-91)

— ❖ —

We now come to the practice of our system of meditation. It is a very simple system, but like all simple systems, it has features of practice which are essential for success. If you put two things together and they create a third thing you have to have both, otherwise the third thing cannot be produced. But if there are twenty factors involved, perhaps one or two could be omitted without much risk of our losing our destination. In yoga there are two elements. There is the self and there is the goal. These two are absolutely essential because without us there is no goal and without the goal there is no need for yoga. This is represented in our system by the Master and the disciple.

The third thing which is necessary is a way to achieve our goal, and that is what the system offers. We sit in meditation. Meditation means just to think constantly about something. Meditation is another word which has been much abused by being considerably obscured but that has all been unnecessary, because meditation only means to think constantly about something. What we think about is what we want to achieve. That is the normal human way. So also in evolution, we have to think about what we are going to achieve. So, it is only a small change from thinking of what we want, to thinking of what we have to become. My Master calls this "diverting the tendencies of the mind to the right direction." So, much effort is not necessary because the power of thought is already in us.

In our daily meditation, we utilize the power of thought which is already in us, to think about the goal which the Master offers. This is the goal of evolution to the highest state of perfection. Now this abstract goal is difficult to meditate upon. It is like the number zero which has no value, but without zero there can be no mathematics. Similarly, we have a goal in our heart which it is difficult to imagine until we achieve it. To make this possible my Master gives us an object of meditation, though it is really not an object, and that is light inside the heart.

We sit comfortably imagining the heart to be filled with this light, and if there are other thoughts which disturb us, we gently avoid or ignore those thoughts. We are told to ignore them because if we apply power to reject them then there is the reaction about which I spoke earlier, and that is the power of that thought to interfere in our meditation. So this is all that we do. The rest, as I have told you, is the third factor in evolution, the Master's transmission to us. That is his business and we leave it to him. (p.102-104)

— ❖ —

The second step is that we have to practise meditation. Meditation is a very simple thing. It means to think continuously about something. Unfortunately, here again there is a great deal of misrepresentation of this term, because most systems treat meditation as concentration. Now, meditation has nothing to do with concentration, at least not in the process. My Master says that meditation is the process that leads to the result which is concentration. The successful practice of meditation leads to concentration. In fact, what we achieve by meditation is a state of mind where the mind can be said to be concentrated. That is, we do not concentrate but our mind is in a state of concentration. ... So, the practice of meditation enables us to achieve finally that state in which we can say the mind is in a state of concentration.

Now in meditation, as I said earlier, we think continuously of something. Meditation is such a universal activity that it is surprising there is so much misunderstanding about it. Because without realising it we are meditating all the time on something or other. A man who is obsessed with the idea of becoming rich is meditating on the idea of wealth. Another person who is obsessed with the idea of being successful in business is similarly meditating on success. But unfortunately, because meditation has been used only in a spiritual context, we do not understand that it is a very commonplace human action, upon which unnecessary esoteric connotations have been brought to bear. Now all that we do in spiritual meditation is simply to change the object from a material object to a spiritual object. And we find that it is very simple and very easy to practise. It is very necessary to realise that meditation is not something foreign to our nature, in which we have to be trained, because meditation is something we are naturally doing all our lives. Only what we have to meditate upon is what we have to achieve. So it is simply a diversion of the mind from its normal activity not even involving a change of direction, but merely a change of the goal that we have to gain. The spiritual goal that my Master offers in this system is the goal of perfection that we can attain. This perfect state is something that is abstract. We do not know what it is until we have achieved it. So my Master has specified for us a simpler goal, a simpler object of meditation which, while serving the purpose of being an object, yet approximates closest to our goal. And that is what we meditate on: light in the heart. My Master says light is the closest to the Ultimate, and therefore it is the most beneficial and effective object on which we should meditate. So this covers the second activity. The first was the cleaning, which I have told you about, the second is the meditation. (p.111-112)

— ❖ —

What we do in spiritual meditation is to try to approach this Ultimate, and the easiest way is to approach it through ourselves, because He resides right here, inside us. (p.118)

— ❖ —

Coming back to the mind and the strengthening of the mind to a stage where we can utilize it fully to achieve all our purposes, Master teaches us a method whereby the mind can be regulated. The first step is the practise of meditation where the mind is put upon a specified exercise. I call it an exercise because the mind is brought to bear upon a single subject, and all intruding or disturbing thoughts are allowed to drop off by non-attention. Non-attention is the greatest weapon to fight thoughts because, my Master says, thoughts without our attention have no power. So, at a single stroke in meditation, by throwing one stone we get two fruits. We train the mind to hold one thought while simultaneously excluding all unnecessary thoughts. ...

When we enter into this practice, we imagine that there is light in the heart, which is the subject of our meditation. There must be some subject, as I have told you, to divert our mind towards a specified channel. The subject is light in the heart. This is the specified approach. And we train the mind by excluding thoughts. My Master says that even with a few months' practice a stage of sufficient concentration is achieved, which we prove in our own experience by achieving moments of almost thoughtless existence. Now a thoughtless state means that there are no disturbing thoughts too because there can be no disturbance without thoughts. This initial achievement makes it possible for us to proceed with greater vigour in our meditation until we come to a final stage where not only in the state of meditation but even in our normal waking state we find that we are capable of being thoughtless for quite substantial lengths of time. Now there are two states of thoughtlessness—one in which we are aware that we are thoughtless and the second state in which we are not even aware that we are thoughtless.

In the latter state something suddenly makes us aware that we have been without a thought for a long time. So this state of thoughtlessness, this state of concentration, we achieve by the practise of a very simple system and with very little effort except to sit in meditation. (p.122-124)

— ❖ —

A second *bhajan* sung by the devotees contains a very important statement, which we should all try to ponder over and understand correctly. That part of the *bhajan* to which I am referring says *yogi hrdyaana gamyam*. One of the meanings of this, as indicated extensively in our ancient literature is, "I am seated in the heart of the yogi and my presence can be experienced by meditation," or, "I enter into the heart of one who does yogic sadhana." According to my Master, what it means is that by the practice of *dhyana* one is able to bring the Almighty Lord into his own heart and enshrine Him there. Thus, by right yoga one becomes a yogi. In this sense, only one who has the Lord in his heart can be rightly called a yogi. Now, since the seat of the Lord is in the heart, my Master says that the Lord should be sought for in one's own heart... (p.152-153)

— ❖ —

Sahaj Marg is a system of meditation, based upon raja yoga, but refined and greatly simplified to suit our time and the condition we live in. It is so simple that it can be practised effectively by any human being. (p.176)

The only manner in which we can test the validity, the applicability or the efficacy of this system of meditation is to participate in its practice and try out what he says. We will then be able to feel whether there is developing in us a sense of peace, an awareness of higher faculties opening up in us, both of which give promise of further growth and expansion in the direction of ultimate Realisation.

Coming to the practical aspect, there are three, and only three, important techniques in the system. The first is meditation. Meditation means to think continuously of one thing. So there is an object upon which we meditate. It is said that, "as we meditate, so we become." Hence the object which is used for meditation must be the correct one to lead us to our goal. My Master says that any object which has grossness or solidity is itself under a limitation. Objects which have inherent limitations cannot be adopted as objects for meditation where the goal is the subtlest one of Realisation. In this system, we meditate upon light in the heart. It is light in an abstract sense, not concretized as light from bulbs or even the sun. He calls the light that we meditate upon, as light without luminosity. It is light but has no luminosity!

The technique is to sit quietly, in a comfortable pose, with eyes closed, having the suggestion in the mind that the heart is internally illuminated by the Higher Presence. We must try to hold this thought continuously. If disturbing thoughts intrude, we are taught to ignore them as something unwanted. Thoughts have no power of their own. They draw power from the attention we give them. So when we ignore unwanted thoughts, they fall off. Should the mind wander from the thought that there is light in the heart, gently bring it back to this thought. Don't use force, for where force is used, a reaction is inevitable. Force creates opposing force. This is the first technique of Sahaj Marg.

(p.177-178)

The Principles of Sahaj Marg, Volume II
Shri P. Rajagopalachari

Our Master has often said that "Prayer is begging whereas meditation is receiving." (p.16)

— ❖ —

In our sadhana, meditation on the heart is prescribed as the means to achieving our *lakshya* or goal. Here too we often find that meditation is done in a very mechanical manner and as Master himself has apologetically pointed out by using a vulgar example, most people meditate as if they are going to the latrine, i.e., when the urge is there, the function is carried out and then forgotten till the need arises again. Sadhana in this sense therefore becomes meaningless and valueless. This means that meditation alone cannot be thought of as sadhana. People who meditate like this have the barest satisfaction of having gone through the process, and become complacent. As Master has pointed out in his *Voice Real*, it is like a man who has got a bit of turmeric and begins to think he is a grocer.

The method of meditation as prescribed in Sahaj Marg is meditation on the heart for half an hour in the morning and half an hour in the evening, and again for a few minutes at bedtime. I am sure that very few people can really say that even this minimum requirement of meditation is being performed by them. Even then the correct way of meditation is to get into the condition which our Divine Master grants us by the power of his transmission, and try to prolong this 'condition' and by thus slowly prolonging it, to ensure that the 'condition' is maintained throughout the twenty-four hours. This is the first stage in our Sadhana. (p.21)

— ❖ —

...We come to the meditative or contemplative paths where sometimes mantras are involved but very often no form of chanting is necessary. This goes by the name of meditation. But even in meditation under traditional raja yoga systems, very often a form is taken up on which to meditate. The Sahaj Marg system teaches that God being an infinite and illimitable entity without graces, attributes and so on, we should really meditate on the abstract principle of divinity and, if this is impossible in the beginning, Master recommends commencement of meditation on light; light being, according to him, the nearest to the abstract. (p.27)

— ❖ —

The only thing that the process of meditation is really meant to teach us is to remind us that there is something above from which we have come here and it is our business to get back where we belong. This is not our home, that is our home. In meditation we experience certain states of existence which make us slowly forget this world. It is not as if we relinquish our hold on this world or we renounce something. In true renunciation we do not renounce anything. The objects which have been enslaving us, they renounce us. It is not we who are attending, it is the whole grasp of our attention which is making us slaves and when our attention goes to something higher, automatically this attraction falls off. Then there is no power in external objects of the world to attract us, to enslave us, to hold us in bondage.

When we start meditation, this memory of our original home is strengthened in us little by little. And as it grows, we find what Master very beautifully calls a state of non-attached attachment. (p.88)

— ❖ —

Every abhyasi has undoubtedly found in his own experience that while he is supposed to be meditating, his mind is wandering where it likes. When he becomes aware of this, the mind is brought back to meditation. This is true of a majority of abhyasis. But there are abhyasis who let their minds wander because it is such a pleasant thing to do. Such persons only 'think' they are meditating. Actually the mind has been let loose to wander at will. Is it any surprise that such abhyasis progress slowly, and some even don't progress at all? If they really meditated when they are supposed to be meditating, results must follow "as the night the day" as the saying goes.

Not satisfied with thus ruining their meditation hour, they destroy their working hours by worrying about lack of progress on the spiritual path. (p.105)

— ❖ —

Many meditate, but few meditate as Master asks us to do. Many only think that they are meditating. Many also use objects of meditation not specified in Sahaj Marg. (p.132)

— ❖ —

When true love for the Master develops, and when one has sufficiently advanced on the spiritual path, a time comes, when the abhyasi sits in meditation, he finds the form of the Master coming to his vision naturally and automatically. I consider this to be the beginning of the true *darshan* of the Master. The form one sees in the heart resembles the physical appearance of the Master, but is no longer the physical form that one sees with the physical eyes. It is but a reflection of that presence. I may say that it is the inner presence of the Master in one's own heart that one sees now. To my mind this is the first real *darshan* of the Master, and it is now appropriate to take up meditation on the Master's form. If meditation is continued along proper lines, a stage comes when the form of the Master fades away even from the inner vision of the abhyasi. The essence comes to one's vision—or I may say that the Master now benevolently blesses the deserving abhyasi with the second stage of his *darshan,* His essence. In the final stages of one's spiritual pursuit one comes into the condition where one finds the Master in His essence, spread out throughout the Universe. This, I believe, is the culmination of one's sadhana. (p.156-157)

The Principles of Sahaj Marg, Volume III
Shri P. Rajagopalachari

We say, "All right, the Master Himself has said, so it must be simple." When we sit in meditation we find we are not really meditating. We are thinking of something else. As someone said, when we sit in meditation the mind is in the office. When we are in the office, some abhyasi comes and we are talking of meditation. We run to our preceptor: "Sahib, how to meditate?" He says "Brother, don't you read the instructions in that small list—one sheet we give you? There are only three things to do. Sit with your eyes closed; imagine there is a Divine light in the heart (it is a mere suggestion); just put your mind over it. It is so simple." We are reassured. We come back and say "Brother... has said, and so and so has said, Master has also confirmed, that it is really simple." "I am a fool, you see, because I have been struggling and I am not able to meditate." We do for three to four days, again we are not able to do something; rush to the preceptors—patient people. Our preceptors are to be praised for their patience, for their dedication. Instead of spending half an hour, he spends two hours, and tells us how simple meditation is: "What, there is nothing else! It is the merest suggestion. Can we not even make the suggestion that there is light in the heart, and put our mind on it?" We say, "Yes sir, it is very simple. I must have been doing something wrong." He says, "Yes. Go and try again." We go home, reinforced by the simplicity of Sahaj Marg. Either we do it or we don't do it, some walk out, some few are fighting it all their lives. (p.2-3)

The Principles of Sahaj Marg, Volume IV
Shri P. Rajagopalachari

Now, meditation means thinking about something continuously. And, what we are supposed to think about here, is Divine light in the heart. So, when an abhyasi says he had too many thoughts or rush of thoughts, in ninety-nine percent of the cases it means that his meditation was on other things than light in the heart. It is not the fault of our system. He was meditating on other things.

Yesterday, I was telling our preceptor brothers and sisters that in the Buddhist tradition there is a story: That one abhyasi was meditating, and you know, they have a supervisor who goes around watching what is going on. The supervisor beat a particular boy, an abhyasi, and told him, "This is not the time to buy fish." He could read the abhyasi's thought that he was sitting in meditation but his thought was in the fish market. Now, this is transferring discipline from the physical sphere to the mental sphere. In the physical sphere, "What we have to do physically?" "Should I put my pen here or here?" Put it in the right place. "Should I leave the door open or closed?" Close it. "Should I flush the bathroom when I leave it?" Flush it. But, what is important to understand is, that if there is no mental discipline, physical discipline cannot exist. That is why we meditate; to achieve regulation over the mind, make it disciplined, make it possible for us to apply the mind where we choose, apply it, not use it, apply it—and thereby achieve a one hundred percent strength of the mind, which makes possible that promise of yoga, that a yogi will be skillful in anything he does.

Indian yogic history does not prove this, if you study the sannyasis. Not because yoga has failed, but because most yogis are yogis in name only; and their minds are wandering much more than the average householder's mind. So, the mind should be regulated by our sadhana; and this can be possible only by the initial discipline of applying it to meditation. This means that a little discipline is first necessary to bring about the bigger discipline and the ultimate discipline. So, this little discipline is what we need, first physically, that little discipline of coming to meditate first; mentally, that little discipline of trying to meditate on what we should be meditating upon; thereby achieving greater and greater, shall I say, regulatory control over our own mind; which leads to greater and greater physical discipline resulting out of that. Because it is the mind which feeds into the body its actions, its desires. Therefore, meditation is the most important activity, if we want to discipline ourselves. (p.116-118)

— ❖ —

So His operation was always from His inner level; we are always operating from the external level. Therefore, we sit for meditation and we think we don't feel anything! Because we are striving for superficial things—experiences, like feeling cold or hot, something crawling on the skin, fear—these are superficial things! You see, they are either at the mental level, or at the mortal level, or even at the physical level! We are not prepared to go in, and then see there where it matters: "What is really happening to you?" Then how can we ever raise ourselves to those levels (those highest levels of spirituality He has referred to), where the Truth resides, where the true experiences reside, where the true proof of the process resides! We are not willing to dive deep. And Babuji has put this in a beautiful allegory: "If you want pearls you must dive to the bottom of the ocean."(p.133)

— ❖ —

...in mysticism they say, "See the Lord with the eyes of the heart; hear Him with the ears of the heart; not with these ears and these eyes. It is impossible." So this is another aspect that we try to develop in our meditation: to develop the perceptivity of what we are trying to perceive—'Light'—in the Divine sense, because God is supposed to have an effulgence, a Divine effulgence. He has no form; so, we don't have a form. He has no name, so, we don't have a *manthra* in our system.

We start with Divine light in the heart, and then we try to see where it leads us. One of the examples or one of the analogies used, in describing the process, is of a diving board which gives you sufficient momentum to dive, but once you have taken off, the board remains behind. It has no further use for us. So, the light in the heart is only a first step. We start off with that and then we have a road here to follow. (p.155-156)

— ❖ —

Because He is us. We call it the Immanent Deity. It is known as mysticism. And therefore we meditate on the inner Deity, not on the external God somewhere in heaven. So, the mystic path has always been the path of meditation. And it is not surprising that when you study the lives of all the great founders of religions, whether it be our Lord Jesus Christ or Buddha, tradition says they all meditated. They meditated and achieved what they had to achieve; or, they became what they had to become. It was by meditation. It was not by ritualistic prayer. It was not in some church or temple. (p.159)

— ❖ —

But we should never forget that there is also a direct path of personal communion with the Ultimate through an act of meditation, which—if you won't misunderstand my saying it—liberates us from religion, too. (p.160)

— ❖ —

You all know about the Roman soldiers who crucified Christ and the effect it had upon them. You know it cannot possibly not have an effect. Like when you put a rose, it must have the perfume (unless I am having a bad cold and I cannot smell!). Similarly these samskaras act as deterrents or blocks, to both the perceptivity of the outside, and the release of my inner love to what is outside. It is a dam. That has to be broken. That we do in meditation. (p.175)

— ❖ —

First, you have to learn to love yourself. That is why perhaps we meditate on our own heart. To find the beauty, however dirty it may be. A beautiful child with mud on its face is not ugly! It has only mud on its face. It is still beautiful. So, the inherent beauty of my heart which the Lord created, cannot be robbed of its beauty, just by a few layers of grossness! Therefore I look within—and as we look at the mirror and say, "Oh, my face is dirty," and have a wash, we wash our hearts. And then we learn to love what we find inside—glittering, glorious—a chamber awaiting the Lord Himself! Then it becomes possible to say, "Master, come! I am now ready for you!"

Because, who would like to invite Master to a dirty place, a filthy place, a corrupt place? That is why, as I say, for meditation on the form, there are so many confusing questions and confused people. Master has said, "Wait till the form appears. Then it is natural to meditate on the form." And, when does the form appear? When He sees, "This heart is now pure enough to accommodate me. Let me enter it; let me accept it; let me reside there now." (p.196)

The Principles of Sahaj Marg, Volume V
Shri P. Rajagopalachari

We meditate half an hour a day and it is as simple as drinking a cup of tea. You sit quietly, comfortably, in such a way that the body does not interfere; you can sit on the chair, you can sit on the floor, as you like; and try to hold your mind on one thought, that there is Divine light in your heart. It is the beginning of acquiring a regulative capacity over one's mind. We train the mind to accept our instruction. This, if you are able to succeed (and it should not take more than a few months), it helps you acquire concentration. (p.70)

There are these famous aphorisms or statements which say, "As you meditate, so you become." You become that on which you meditate. Think of God, you become God. Think of stone, you become a stone. Therefore, we start with this idea of light in the heart, because as I said, God can have no form or name. Therefore we have no *manthras*, we have no *ishta devatas*, as we think of in the Hindu Religion—worshipping Christ or worshipping Rama or Krishna or Buddha or anything like that. It is an abstraction. But the human mind cannot comprehend the abstract, at least not in the beginning. So my Master says, light in the heart is the most abstract concept that you can have. It has no form, it has no substance, it has no weight. So from that as the starting point, as our meditation goes deeper and deeper, it reveals to us from within ourselves—by the grace of the Almighty and by our efforts, it is a conglomerate of two things—who God is or what true Divinity means. And, there must come a time when one day we can say, "I have an inkling of what it is, not because I have seen it, or touched it but because I have felt it." Now people don't understand why this should not be so. Why should we not 'see' God? We don't see sorrow, we feel sorrow. We feel hungry. I mean, almost every important thing in our lives, we feel, we experience. This is the most transcendental experience of all, that I feel Divine, because I am Divine. So Divinity—God—cannot be the object of knowledge, cannot be the object of perception, cannot be revealed by perception. But, as my Master said, when we meditate, and the meditation is right and successful as it must be, we progressively draw whatever we can from the Divine Source, by progressively divinising ourselves; yet at no stage can that person say, "I am God." You may be like God in every way, in every quality, in everything that you can imagine; yet God is God and you continue to be the humble devotee—no doubt divinised to the highest possible extent—nevertheless, "He is what He is, I am what I am!"

(p.71-72)

So, we have all been saying, "God is Love; God is humane; God is merciful." And then we practise uncharitable things and talk of punishment. So, that is the contradiction in practice which we have to set right, and try to infuse in our heart (where He is already residing in a minute atomic form) this love for Him, in an act of meditation where we surrender ourselves, our activities and say, "Lord, sit within me, that I shall become you." This is the substance of spirituality. (p.73)

The Principles of Sahaj Marg, Volume VI
Shri P. Rajagopalachari

So when we meditate without the positive idea that we have to reach a destination, that there is a goal in front of us, we are on one of these merry-go-round trips. It is no different from a drug. So we go round and round—"Round and round the mulberry bush," as there is a poem in English. Then what do we get out of it, not even a mulberry! We are stuck; so if you want to move in a straight line, you have got to keep the idea of a destination in view. (p.46)

— ❖ —

...even the great rishis, even the gods, they have to use the mind in doing this thing that we call *tapas*, meditation, *dhyan*. But if, in that process desire comes and says, "Ask for powers, ask for the *Brahmaastra*, ask for the beautiful damsels of heaven," well, the power of the fruit of the *tapas* cannot be denied to you and they say, '*Tathastu*" and we are left with that. So my Master always said, "Regulate the mind so that even desires at that stage should not rise." (p.141)

...if you want to train the body you have to indulge in physical exercise; if you want to regulate the mind, it has to be trained by repeated practice and that is all that meditation is about. The average human being is afraid of the word meditation; he is afraid of the word *tapasya*; he says, "Oh! That is only for the rishis. How can we, mere ordinary mortals, living an ordinary life, how can we do it?" (p.142)

— ❖ —

Now how to do it. You sit in meditation because meditation means thinking of one thing continuously for a length of time. It is no more than that. And my Master used to emphasize that this is a childish thing, which every child does. You know, a child wants a bag of sweets or a packet of biscuits, it won't give up that thought until it gets it. You are all familiar with children. It wants a toy, well, it never forgets the toy. Even through sleep it remembers and next morning says, "Where is this toy I had asked for?" Even a child is able to meditate on some thing. So what is it that we are required to do? We are only required to change the object of meditation. Because spiritual science says, "That on which you meditate, that you become." So if you meditate on wealth, you become wealthy; you meditate on health, you become healthy; because the continuous flow of the mind in that particular direction seems to attract that which you seek towards yourself. So all that spirituality says is: change the object of meditation into that which you call perfection, which you call the human level of the highest evolution, which in simple words, is Divinisation.

Now comes the question, "Well, I am prepared to meditate on Divinity. How do I meditate on the Divine?" My Master says, "So long as you meditate on limited forms, limited names, there is a limitation. The moment you say Shiva, he is only a Shiva, may be, with the *trishul* and this and that and the snake around the neck. ... Now how to meditate on the Ultimate which has no name, no form, no attribute? My Master said, "**Meditate on**

light."—*'Ishwariya prakash'* in the heart as something which is a 'pointer' to His existence in the heart, because the heart is supposed to be the seat of the Divine, in the human system, as in all other systems.

...So this is the process, that we sit comfortably, imagine light in the heart—the Divine light in the heart—and try to hold that thought for as long as we can. If the mind wanders, gently bring it back, so that eventually (Eventually need not be a frightening word, that it takes centuries depends on us! Eventually can mean today, eventually can mean three months, eventually can mean thirty years.) we have the capacity to keep the mind on that one thought alone, then we find that concentration is developed.

(p.143-145)

— ❖ —

But the inner penetration into the uttermost depths of your being is not something that can be achieved by technology or science. It can only be achieved by negating the self. "I don't need vision; let me close my eyes"—this is what we do in meditation. "I don't need to hear; so let me listen to the voice of the Master from within"—that doesn't need any ears. "I don't need knowledge; let me forget my intellect." "I don't need strength; let me lose myself in my meditation and forget that I have a body." So, what are we left with? We are left with the 'Self' looking into itself. At the same time it is a very silly thing, any fool can do it. As Babuji used to say, "*har bewakoof kar sakta hai*." And the "*bewakoof*" is able to do it easier than the wise man or the wise woman precisely because the wise one thinks that it is wisdom which is taking us somewhere; the fool knows, "I have no wisdom, I have no wealth, I have no strength, I have nothing, I am dependent on Him who is inside me. Let me seek Him inside." Therefore, if you are able to persuade a village idiot to sit and meditate—idiot in the sense not of a brain-damaged idiot, but an *unpad* idiot, unlettered, untutored, simple man—he becomes a saint almost instantly. (p.159-160)

I don't think an artist can ascribe to himself or herself any more credit than a businessman who has earned crores of rupees. They are both using human faculties—one in this direction and the other in that direction. All that I would like to suggest is **use it also to go inside**. Make the tree firm. Push its roots down to the uttermost possible depths that we can achieve. And this we achieve in meditation. Because the externally directed senses, the externally penetrating powers that we are endowed with, by Divine grace, by Nature, by heredity, well, they guarantee a certain amount of success in the outside world. To retain it, to consolidate it, to make it noble, grand, perfect—**reach in**, balance it by a **plunge into** the innermost depths of yourself, anchor yourself to Him who is there and then you find that you can fly beyond the greatest flights, even of Divinity itself. This is the secret I alluded to briefly in my talk the day before yesterday, that perhaps Brahma, Vishnu, and Shiva were people who meditated like us. (p.169-170)

The Principles of Sahaj Marg, Volume VII
Shri P. Rajagopalachari

Babuji Maharaj always said, "Just because you sit comfortably, and close your eyes for forty-five minutes or one hour, it doesn't mean you are meditating." He would also tell a joke—not a joke but a very serious thing in the form of a joke—that when people sit for meditation, they think of the price of rice, the election results, all sorts of things! Lalaji once told one of his disciples that the price of a bag of rice is not eight rupees but six rupees, because the man who was supposed to be meditating was only thinking of rice! So just because everybody is sitting with eyes closed, doesn't mean that everybody is meditating.

This is one thing that we have all got to understand, that when people have been meditating for so many years and they are not making any progress, there must be some reason. Of course it is always easy to blame the system, blame the Master, because nobody wants to blame himself! ... So Babuji always used to feel very sorry that people say, "Babuji! I am not progressing. I have been with you for fifteen years or twenty years, and why am I not progressing?" Babuji used to say, "The answer is obvious. Look inside yourself. Are you meditating? Are you doing the cleaning?" Sometimes he used to tell me, "Occasionally, I take the risk of asking them this question, 'How often do you meditate?' And people used to say, 'Babuji, not regularly, but at least two or three times a week!' 'Do you do the cleaning?' Many people said, 'We do not have enough time for cleaning.' So, if you are meditating two or three times a week, and you have no time for cleaning at all, how are you going to make any progress? I suppose, only the Master can answer. Perhaps, even he could not answer, because there was no answer. (p.1-2)

— ❖ —

"...once you start something, you will feel something; once you feel something you will go on so that you can do it, and benefit from it." That was the theme. It doesn't mean you are going to achieve. It is like Babuji saying in *Voice Real*: "Can you not spare five minutes for this insignificant being?" Does it mean that by five minutes meditation a day, you are going to be a saint? If somebody is going to quote *Voice Real* and say Babuji has said that—excuse me, but he is very foolish. It is like putting a drop of milk in the child's mouth, making it open the mouth, and then putting its feed up. It is eliciting co-operation in some way... Therefore Babuji said, "Meditate one hour; can't you do it? meditate half an hour; can't you do that? meditate at least fifteen minutes; no, even if that is not possible for you, my dear brother, can you not spare at least five minutes for this insignificant being?" Now, if people believe that by meditating for five minutes a day, and after that, not doing the cleaning, and then putting the whole responsibility on the Master, we can progress—yes, there may be one-in-a-million case who will progress.

Not because he is meditating for five minutes or anything like that, but because of his faith, and belief, and then devotion, to the Master. At least **that** we should have! And if you are not able to practise, at least you should try to develop love for the Master, faith in the Master. As Babuji said, "Three things we must have: satsangh with the Master, obedience to the Master, love for the Master."

So, we have to have patience, you see. It is not enough to just practise. I practise because of my obedience to the Master. Am I thinking of light in the heart for one hour, as I am supposed to when I sit for meditation? This is the first question we should ask ourselves. Obedience is not enough, is not sufficient. It is not compliance, by just sitting with eyes closed and thinking about the price of rice, and saying, "Babuji! I do sit for one hour with my eyes closed." Are you meditating?

So when you meditate like this for one hour and really meditate, you are hitting two birds with one stone; satsangh with the Master and obedience to the Master—two things. Isn't it? Third thing will develop because of our *sahavasa* (association) with the Master inside our heart. The more we internalize our thought, the more we internalize our attention, we begin to love **that** which we see inside us. Of course, that which He is externally, is also lovable, but we find this more so. Then comes Love. After that, a stage comes, when we can even give up meditation.

You will not think that I am saying something unnecessary when I say that, in 1972 Babuji told me, "You don't have to meditate any more." Meditation is no longer necessary because meditation is also a process. It is not an aim in itself, it is not an end in itself, that you continue meditating all your life. Of course, if the guru says, "Continue," you continue. It is like eating. We eat enough. Just because something is good, we don't sit at the table and go on eating all day!

So, first of all, we must remember that meditation is a process. It is a process which we undertake to reach a destined goal, a predetermined goal. I don't say, "Well, this train is going; let me go wherever it goes! I will end up in Howrah instead of Vijaywada, and there also I will get down only because the train has reached a junction or a terminus." So, obedience means doing when he says "Do;" stopping when He says "Stop." (p.6-8)

— ❖ —

We are going to **one** goal. We are following the same marg, and we are all heading for what we think is one destiny for us. So, that is the first important thing for promoting brotherhood. Second, that when we sit and meditate, hundred or two hundred people, it has much more capacity to draw the Divine towards us, or the grace of the Divine towards us, than when one person meditates. Combined effort is much more than the multiplication of the individual effort.

...We obey the Master because we wish to go somewhere, achieve some destination, achieve some goal. Therefore I have to obey him. He says, "Today you meditate one hour," I meditate one hour. He says, "Sit again after five minutes," I sit again after five minutes. (p.10)

— ❖ —

Well, I don't think any of you or any of us, anywhere in this world today, are able to meditate for somebody else's sake. We are meditating for our sake. Each one is on his or her way on this marg, for his personal or her personal evolution to the highest. (p.13-14)

— ❖ —

Many people think, that just because we meditate regularly, just because we do cleaning regularly, just because we are devoted to Master, we have a right to the goal you know, some sort of *haq* (right). I would like to disillusion you of this idea. However dedicated our practice, however sincere our approach, we have no right to the goal. It is His grace that He gives us this. Babuji used to tell me again and again, "Only he receives to whom He wishes to give." (p.20)

When we meditate, thinking that, "We are doing something and he is bound to give us something," we are behaving like labour and management. My statement of demands: "Master, I have been meditating one hour every day regularly; I have been cleaning every day regularly; I have been devoted to you, I have loved you; where is my reward?" It becomes a commercial transaction. Love cannot be a transaction. (p.21)

— ❖ —

You know, I am reminded of a boy, a new abhyasi. I think in *Reality at Dawn* Babuji has written, "If anybody wants to know who is the Special Personality, let him meditate with a sincere prayer in his heart that 'He may be revealed', and He will surely appear before him." This abhyasi wanted to know who the Special Personality is. Now, if I tell him it is Babuji, he will say, "How do you know?" So I said, "Meditate. The method is given in the book." After one week, he came running and said, "Sir, what is this?" Every time I meditate with this question, only Babuji's form appears!" Have you understood? The boy had decided Babuji is **not** the Special Personality! Now, however many times the form may appear, he says, "What is this? Every time I sit, Babuji appears!" Babuji Maharaj has said, "You sit and meditate with this question in your heart and the form will appear." (p.27)

— ❖ —

I told you this morning that, "Don't **think** you meditate—but **meditate**." (p.41)

— ❖ —

Because we are something and we can be made into something, therefore He comes to help us. So we have to meditate, we have to do the cleaning. His assistance is there. (p.42-43)

So if you think, "Grace is automatic, meditation He will do, cleaning He will do," then why should **I** be here at all? I need not have been born. He would have seen that I don't have to be taking birth. Don't you think so? Babuji said, "You take one step and I will not fail in taking one step." But your step is eighteen inches, His step is *saptaloka*! (all the seven worlds). (p.44)

— ❖ —

But you know, you have to call a doctor when you are sick. The doctor doesn't go around asking, "Well, is there anybody sick here?" Isn't it? **You** have to bring him to your house. So that "bringing Him to the house" is meditation. (p.47)

— ❖ —

...God helps those who help themselves. I must eat, He helps me digest the food. "No, no if God wishes He will keep me alive, Sir." So will you stop eating? I would suggest that all those who don't want to meditate and say Master does everything, let them also not eat—*visha pariksha* (acid-test). Why not? (p.48)

— ❖ —

Only for meditation we have this hypocritical attitude, that, "He does, who are we to do?" But when it is business, when it is my wife's sickness, when it is my son's marriage, we run like mad people here and there. So you have a right to talk of Master, His greatness, His power, only when you have one attitude to everything—not one for yourself and one for others. For meditation and cleaning, "Babuji will do;" for everything else, "I will do." Is it fair? You examine your heart. How many of you are willing to say, "From today I shall not eat." (p.49)

— ❖ —

I have had abhyasis coming to me, "Sir, if your Master is so powerful, why doesn't He make me meditate?" Don't you think it is a stupid way of testing the Master? So remember, God helps those who help themselves. (p.50)

— ❖ —

You know, in the Christian tradition it says, "Ask and it shall be given to you; seek and ye shall find; knock and it shall be opened." But when you think you already know who is the Special Personality, who is God, what is this, what is that, and if you ask somebody, he will only laugh at you. "My friend, when you know the answer, why do you ask me?" "No, no, but is it the right answer?" Well, sit down and meditate on it, and when the answer comes, if you want a confirmation, do it again. Do it a third time. But beyond that, if you do, it is like trying to milk a bull, you see! You get nothing but a sore in the fingers!

So, even for asking the question, Babuji has given such a simple and wonderfully effective technique, which anybody can practise anywhere. (p.58)

— ❖ —

So you see, the sole and only totally effective practice to keep us on the straight and narrow path without deviation, without problems arising, without any embarrassing situation being created, is constant remembrance. Because the mind is better occupied, it cannot wander here and there. See, that is why Master has recommended it so much, even beyond meditation. Meditation is only a process. Constant remembrance is superior to meditation. If one can be involved in constant remembrance, then there is no need to meditate. Now, even constant remembrance has a purpose—to create love for the Master. Once you love him so much that there is nothing else in the universe you can possibly love, even constant remembrance becomes unnecessary, because now love has taken its place. Then we obey Him, His principles, His teachings—not because it is some imposition of the Lord, or some authority that He has established Himself to be, but because we love Him. We wish to please Him with everything that we do. We wish to become what He is, or what He wants us to become. Therefore surrender comes naturally. From meditation, to constant remembrance, to love, to surrender—these are the four stages of our evolution. Unfortunately, most of us, we make a very weak attempt at meditation—not even real meditation. ...

What can prevent my grossness from being acquired? It is constant remembrance. How to acquire it? By meditation. What is meditation? Thinking continuously of one thing. What is that one thing that we should think of? Divine light in the heart—not our preceptor, however wonderful he may be; not the wife, however much we may love her; not even the form, because we don't know what form He has, if any, whether He exists, if at all He does. (p.81-83)

— ❖ —

The secret is go into the Self, see the Master there, eternally bind Him to yourself and then relax. Where can He go now? He has to go everywhere I go! If I sit, He sits. If I speak He is still inside me looking after me. It is said that, you know, karma, how does it protect us? When we are awake, we are conscious enough to look after ourselves—or at least so we think, though very often we find we cannot do even that! Who looks after us when we are asleep? He, who is ever present.

Now, He who is ever present is only a concept for us. It is not a reality. Because we use Him, as Babuji Himself said—excuse me if I tell you something which I shouldn't say, I mean the words He used, you see—"People meditate like going to the toilet. At need. When the pressure in the stomach is unbearable we rush to the toilet, make use of it, flush it, and walk out." He said, "This is how we use the Master, how we use meditation." "Oh! Babuji! Today I am in trouble. My boss fired me in the office. So I sit and meditate for ten minutes, so that the pain of that encounter would go away." My son is seriously sick, with tears in my eyes I sit and meditate, "Master, help me." What is the use? He who must be ever present in me, part of myself—my **self**—we are relegating to some place, whether it be in Shahjahanpur or Timbuktu—and trying to reach Him when we need, you see! At that moment, are we in the capacity to call Him, have we the capacity to bring Him to us? (p.121-122)

— ❖ —

Now, Babuji has said, "Have a special place for meditation, have a special *asan*, have a special time." It is creating an environment into which, as you come, automatically we get into the meditative, contemplative mood. So, that particular spot that we reserve for meditation, you can say, is an ashram too. There is an old saying, that where a king lives, is a palace. He may come to your house tomorrow morning, just unannounced. For him it is a palace. It is not the other way round, you see. What the king sits on, is a throne. It may be specially made, it may be gold, it may be just wood.

So, let us not confuse principles with actuality, reality, and try to bestow material things upon reality, which is lacking, but try to preserve that pristine purity, which our Master has blessed us with. People often ask, "What is the need for Him to come again and again?" I think it was only to renew that Presence of His, by the physical presence of His own. He came, He saw what was to be corrected, He rectified the atmosphere, purified it, perhaps charged it, if necessary and when necessary. That was for our benefit, like we charge a battery. Every so often, a battery needs to be charged. Who does the charging? Well, the Master does the charging. It is like the first charge of the first new battery that you buy. But then, subsequently, it is our job to keep that charge by doing our meditation properly, by sitting in an attitude of contemplation, sitting in an attitude of devotion, dedication to the principles of the Mission, in a real spirit of an abhyasi.

(p.132-133)

Then, he again fell at my feet and wept and said, "Brother, do something for me, remove this defect in me." I asked him, "Do you believe I can do it?" He said, "You are Master's Representative. It cannot be that you cannot do it." Then I said, "All right, sit in meditation." I gave him a sitting for twenty minutes. He was a changed man after that.

Why I am saying this is—suppose somebody has a doubt, either they should meditate and request Master to bless them with the knowledge, or they can come to me and ask me to give them a sitting and see if it is not cleaned off. How can you help anybody who is not willing to try both? (p.148-149)

— ❖ —

...and here we are playing with meditation for half an hour a day, twenty minutes a day, fifteen minutes a day, and talking of the Central Region! Babuji was very emphatic, that all our sadhana can do, is to attract His attention towards us. Unless that attention is attracted, we get nothing. (p.165)

The Principles of Sahaj Marg, Volume VIII
Shri P. Rajagopalachari

Is it the practice which is important, or the Master who is important? If the Master says, "You go into the kitchen and cook," you say, "No, no, Babuji, I have to meditate you know, why don't you send somebody else? There are five thousands abhyasis here." Babuji says, "Yes, it is all right, you sit in meditation, I will send somebody else." Can you benefit by such meditation? Meditation is no more and no less than a patient lying on the table of the doctor. He makes himself available. Then the Master works on him, like the surgeon who operates. Now, if at the time when you have to be on the table of the doctor, you say, "No, no, I have to be in the cinema hall," the doctor says, "Come tomorrow." Now, when you are doing the Master's work, His attention is always on you. If you are only working on yourself, occasionally He may think of you. You see even at home if your carpenter is working, every two minutes you leave your work and go and see that the carpenter is working properly, what he is doing, giving instructions. Don't you attend to the carpenter? You give him tea, you look after his needs. Those who work for us are more important to us than those who just sit. (p.8)

— ❖ —

We are all proud talking of the book *Towards Infinity*. But when we go towards infinity, we want it to be a limited infinity. "No, no, sir, after all fifteen years of practice, how much more should I do? Have I to still go on meditating?" Yes, because you have not seen. If you can see on the very first day, your sadhana stops right there. As Babuji said, "Turn your head from here to there and the job is done." But we are not able to turn our head, you know. "Yes, yes, I am going to turn my head, please wait! Let me look at this beautiful thing in front of me." And we are seeing the beautiful thing and forgetting the reality here.

(p.106)

— ❖ —

So as He puts more and more of Himself into us, we become more and more of what Master is. When we experience these states, expanding states, deepening states, when we say in our experience, "Today the meditation was very deep. I felt plunged into some bottomless place," or "I felt myself expanding beyond my body;" these are the states of experience that are given to us by the Master, by His pouring Himself, His essence into us. And now this can only be possible if I meet with an open heart, with an open mind and say, "Lord! Whatever I am, there is still more you can give me. Even when I am like Brahma and Vishnu and Shiva!" (p.108)

Well, the first step is to close your eyes, you see. Because when we open the eyes we see the external world. When we close the eyes, we can divert our attention now to our own inner self. Therefore in meditation we have always to close our eyes, even the great *tapasvis* of the past, you can see they were sitting in the *asana* with their eyes closed, their attention centred on their heart. Many systems preach attention on the forehead or navel, but we meditate on the heart for the important reason that the heart is the seat of life, the seat of existence of Divinity. So you see, this is what I would like to say about spirituality, that the external search is not only for material pleasures, material welfare, material growth, material success and trying to evade the inexorable end of a material existence, which is a material death. (p.116)

— ❖ —

Now we just meditate for twenty minutes, fifteen minutes, ten minutes, perfunctory cleaning in the evenings, prayer meditation at night. Who does (prayer meditation), I don't know. And then we are troubled when we have no progress, and we say, "Well, I thought Babuji was merciful. I thought He was compassionate." That is the ultimate indignity we confer on the Master, that we doubt. As Babuji said, "Doubt poisons the will." The moment we begin to doubt, the will is lost. After that we cannot sit in meditation. "*Man nahin lagta hai*" (I don't feel inclined). "*Kaise lagega?*" (How will you be inclined?) When the mind is doubting the Master? "*Ham pooja mein baithte hain*" (I am sitting in meditation), will He do this or not? "*Woh denge ya nahin?*" (Will He give or not?) You see, you are not meditating, you are doubting. So whenever people come and say, "*Saab, man nahin lagta hain, ham dhyan nahin kar paten hain*" (Sir, I don't feel inclined to do meditation, I am not able to meditate), it is a manifestation of their doubt in the Master, in the system, because otherwise the mind is an instrument, why should it not? As Babuji said, "*Man lagta nahin hain, man ko lagana padta hain.*" (Mind does not feel inclined, mind is made to feel inclined.)

Otherwise you don't have to sit in meditation. Meditation is a training to apply the mind for the purpose of regulating the mind by our efforts. If it is automatically regulating itself, why should we meditate? We are already rishis! So that is the idea, you see, that when doubt comes, our will power goes, we are not able to use the mind. As Babuji said, the whole purpose of meditation is to make a reversal in this fact of life that the mind is our Master. We have to become the Master of our mind. *Bas itna hi hain. Palat do.* (It is only this much, just reverse it.) But this we have to do, you know. It is like riding a horse. You have to ride it and train it. You cannot show a book and say, "Allow me to ride you properly. This is what a good horse should be!" You have to ride, you have to risk being thrown a few times, you have to ride it gently, but with total control over its reins. You must be kind, yet you must be firm. (p.130-131)

— ❖ —

Similarly that which I am evolving towards is my source, not my goal. See it is mistakenly called the goal. We call 'goal', but as an expedient term by which to define it—really it is the source. Therefore Master calls it the Original Home from which we have come; the memory of which we have lost; the cause of which is ever present in our heart, as the timely voice of conscience; and which, if you will meditate, gets stronger and stronger. (p.150-151)

— ❖ —

Now one thing I discovered very early, that most of these great religious teachers were meditating in the morning. We get up very early in the South, like the Bengalis, and I used to find these swamijis, the Shankaracharyas, from three o'clock, sometimes from half past two, they were sitting in meditation, but afterwards after six o'clock when their own meditation was over and their *bhaktas* (devotees) started coming to my house to have *darshan*, they used to be given *prasad* in the form of fruits, coconuts, the *teertha* as we call it, the holy water and there was *pravachan* about the Bhagavad Gita, the Ramayana. And this hiatus between what they were doing for themselves and what they were offering to their devotees was a bit of a shock to me. In fact I was, shall I say, rude enough or forward enough to question one Shankaracharya in my father's presence at the age of twelve. I said "Swamiji, you are doing something for yourself and you are giving us something else, however holy it might be. Don't you think it is rather unfair that the special practice is reserved for yourself and you are just passing us off with some *prasad*?" My father was very annoyed, I had a beating for it. But that was no answer.

Next morning I approached the Shankaracharya again. He said, "My son, what you are asking is a legitimate question, but you know you have to pass through many *janmas* (births) of practice, association with holy people, the preliminaries, the kindergarten stuff, before you can be fit for meditation." I said "Why? How many lives have you passed before you became a Shankaracharya. Do you know it? Have you a record of your past?" He said, "No, it is not possible." I said, "Well, Lord Krishna says in the Bhagavad Gita that it is possible to know one's past life. He says, 'I know all my past existences, not only that, I know all my future existences too,' and He says, 'I taught what I am teaching you to the *manus* of the past.' So it is not impossible." He said, "Well if one can become a Lord Krishna, perhaps it is possible." I said, "Then I come to the next question: How do you know this is not your first life in which you have started meditation itself straight away? Why do you assume that you have had past existences in which you have done *pujas* and *kriyas* and *acharas* and *niyamas*." There was no answer.

The answer came to me in a very delightfully simple and encouraging fashion when I came to my Master, Shri Ram Chandraji Maharaj of Shahjahanpur. I asked Him this question: "How many lives of preparation do we need?" "It is a human weakness," that's what my Master said. It is a human weakness to imagine that we have to prepare ourselves for meditation. Meditation itself is a process which prepares us to receive the grace of the Almighty through preparation of the mind, conditioning of the mind, regulation of the mind, because the mind is the most potent thing that we have. The mind either ruins us or the mind makes us. (p.155-157)

— ❖ —

So you see it is a progressive, shall we say, hardening, like we have hardening of the arteries as we grow old. There has been a progressive hardening, but you find the spiritual tradition of meditation, *tapasya* as the Upanishad calls it, alive even into this century when we have the great Ramakrishna Paramhansa for instance here in this land of Bengal. You all know his life. He started as a *pujari* in the Kali Temple right here in Dakshineshwar and through his puja he achieved a certain stage where they say he was able to meet with Kali *mata* in a very personal physical way where he used to talk with her, play with her, treat her as his mother, she loved him as her son and he seemed to have attained some sort of a *samadhi*. But later comes the second and the more glorious half which made Ramakrishna the *pujari* into Ramakrishna Paramhansa. When Totapuri came into his life and taught him how to do *nirvikalpa samadhi,* he said, "What is this you are doing? Are you happy with this, are you satisfied with this? However great Kali may be, yet she is only Kali. There is a limitation here. Transcend it." (p.159)

— ❖ —

Today we have come to such a stage where we have to pretend that it is necessary to have a hundred life times to be able to meditate.

My Master said that it is the most single, weakening idea that has pervaded the human Indian mind that meditation is an impossible thing. I said, "Master, how do you say this?" He said, "Well, if a man is obsessed with the idea of making money and thinks of nothing but money twenty-four hours of the day, is he not meditating on the money, because the definition of meditation is to think continuously of something. If you are thinking continuously of money, you are doing meditation on money and every occult spiritual tradition says that on which you meditate, that you shall become. It is no wonder that a man who meditates on money becomes a millionaire. It is no wonder, a man who is obsessed with success becomes a success. But should it be a wonder if a man, obsessed with the idea of God, becomes like God? We say, "Yes, it is not possible." Spirituality says, "Yes, it is possible. Try it and see."

...We have the Sapta-Rishis, we have untold unknown rishis who prevailed this land. We have the greatest figures like Yagnavalkya for instance, Vashistha, Vishwamitra who were in the jungle, who did *tapasya*. *Tapasya* means sitting in the cross-legged pose and meditating on God. Is it only for the old people?

(p.161-162)

— ❖ —

Even Patanjali defines asana as a posture which one adopts for the period of meditation, maybe for an hour, maybe for two hours, and it is defined by Patanjali himself as: *"Sthira sukham asanam"*—that which can be held comfortably, that which can be held steadily over the period of time that one wishes to meditate, that is asana. Now during meditation, the frequency of breathing automatically adjusts itself. This has been the universal experience of all our practitioners, abhyasis, that as we slip into or glide deeper and deeper into meditation, the breathing cycle slows down very considerably and I have myself experienced that at one point or at one stage during the meditation, one becomes almost breathless. Well, it is not right to call it breathlessness but there is a cessation of breath and this cessation of breath can last almost indefinitely. I have experienced it sometimes for two minutes, three minutes and once as much as six and a half minutes, because my Master timed it and said, "Do you know that you were breathless or without breathing for six and a half minutes today?" Then he explained to me that only by this practice could the yogis of the past practise this often-talked-about thing that they were buried underground for two days or six days or forty days where there is no air, no oxygen. It was by the suspension of breathing, not by storing oxygen in their lungs or any such thing.

So, *pranamaya* is a result of meditation. It adjusts itself to the requirements of the system, of the spiritual system and unfortunately *pranamaya* cannot create that state, which is created by meditation only. So this is something which must be understood that *pranamaya* is a result in the sense that a meditative state or a contemplative state results in a state of lower intake of oxygen and breathing but per contra the breathing cycle cannot induce a state of contemplation or deep meditation. (p.172-173)

— ❖ —

So these first four steps, my Master cut off as it were, as not only unnecessary but impractical in modern times. It takes years and years of practice to achieve such contemplative state—that is what the Patanjali Yoga Sutra says. Once when I was abroad, I had the privilege of going to one of the other (Indian) Missions abroad. There I found a foreign lady, a French lady I think, who had been in that particular Mission for a period of twenty years. My Master was talking to the Head of that Mission and I was walking around in the garden, speaking to this lady and I said, "How often and how long do you meditate every day?" She said, "Meditation! I can't do it yet. " I said, "What do you mean you can't do it? You have been here for twenty years and don't you think that you are qualified enough to meditate?" She said, "No, no, Mr. Chari, you know I have been in the nursery for three years, then I was in the kitchen for three years, then I have been in the garden for three years and then in the laundry for three years. Swamiji says I have to go on like this perfecting each aspect of the material existence before I can be fit enough to meditate."

Now later on when I came out with my Master, I asked Babuji, as we used to affectionately call him, "What is this? These people are teaching that we have to have twenty-five years or forty years of preparation for meditation?" He said, "This is the stupidity. They are teaching people that we have to learn to meditate, but we can learn to meditate only by meditating!"

You see for a moment it was a little difficult for me to understand this but later on I understood that one learns to bicycle only by riding a bicycle. One does not learn the theory on the ground and then step on the bicycle and master it instantly. One learns to ride a horse by riding a horse. Of course, there is always the danger of being thrown off and we have to be prepared for it. So meditation itself teaches us how to meditate. That is where we start from.

Right from day one, we start with meditation, and my Master says we should adopt for meditation the subtlest thing that we can possibly adopt, because God is the subtlest thing in creation, if you will have it, though He is Himself the Creator. So in this system, we meditate on light in the heart as the subtlest thing that we can possibly adopt. We do not advocate or recommend the name of God or a form of God because every form and every name becomes a limitation. And a limited concept can only lead to a limited goal and to a limited realisation of that goal. Therefore we adopt, in this system of Sahaj Marg, meditation on light in the heart, because it is in the heart that the Divine presence is supposed to be there. In all religions it is an accepted fact. So we seat the Divinity as it were in an invisible form in the heart and meditate on the effulgence that flows out of that presence, imagining that the heart is illuminated from inside. This is substantially what we do during meditation. (p.173-175)

— ❖ —

Q: Why does Sahaj Marg recommend meditation on the heart?

A: This is an important question because in yogic literature we find that meditation has been recommended on the point of the nose, on the point between the eyebrows and several other points. For instance in the Bhagavad Gita, Lord Krishna himself says, "*Bhruvormadhye pranamaveshya samyak*"—"Bring your life resources in terms of prana to the point between the eyebrows and meditate on that." But in Sahaj Marg, we meditate on the light in the heart. The light is located in the heart. My Master has explained that there are three very important reasons for this.

The first is that, the heart is the seat of Divinity in the human system, as in all other systems. This is something which is universally accepted. All religions seat the Lord in the heart, not in the head or in the stomach but in the heart. So when you want to approach Divinity through your system, you approach Him by His presence in your heart, which is known as the *antaryamin*—one who resides within. The Gita says, the Lord says in the Gita: "I am in the heart of every created being." So it has not only scriptural authority, it has a sort of universal authority because it is something in which all humanity believes, that if the Lord resides anywhere, it is in our heart.

Secondly, we describe the human being by his heart. For instance we use terms such as: "He is a kind hearted person" or "She is a cold hearted woman" or "He has a soft heart" or "He has a bitter heart" or "His heart is as black as coal" or somebody's heart is hard as stone. So human qualities, human character is defined by the heart. This is how the human being is treated. If the heart is there, he exists. If he doesn't, it is gone.

The third important reason is that the human life itself seems to be centred in the heart, because everything else can fail, you can cut off a man's hands and legs, you can cut off his fingers, you can cut off his nose, but if the heart stops, everything stops. That is another important reason.

The fourth very important reason according to my Master is that when we concentrate on the heart or meditate on the heart, we are in a sense affecting the whole system in a total way because the blood circulation starts and ends with the heart.

Everything goes round the system from the heart, pumped out from the heart, comes back to the heart purified through the lungs. And therefore we purify the heart, put love into the heart, which is what we try to do in Sahaj Marg. It is, in a sense, trying to make pervasive the application of a unique force, the power of love, the power of the Master's spiritual attainment into the heart, from where it spreads through the whole system.

So these are the very important reasons why we meditate on the heart in the Sahaj Marg system. One, as I said it is the seat of Divinity. Two, as I said it is that by which the human life, the human character is defined. Three, it is that which governs life, in that if it is there, we exist, if it stops we cease to exist. And fourth, it is the point from which the blood circulation starts and stops. You know blood is a very vital constituent of the human system because it is that which carries nourishment to every part of the body, brings back the waste products of existence, circulates it through the lungs, purifies and then recirculates it all over again through the system. So the heart and blood form a very vital part or component of our existence and if the purification is carried out here, it is pervading throughout the system. So these are the four important reasons. (p.180)

— ❖ —

In Sahaj Marg spiritual training, constant remembrance is a very important step in one's evolution. I should perhaps start off by answering that we have meditation at the first step; through meditation we are reminded of our goal, because we meditate on the Divine light in the heart. The more we meditate, the more the remembrance of what my Master calls the original home is reinforced and the reinforcement of that memory creates a longing in us to go back to that home. So I think meditation essentially is a technique to create a remembrance of what we come from, where we have descended from, our home, our parents. So remembrance, in my understanding, is the result of meditation.

(p.187-188)

You say, "From tomorrow, I get up early to do my morning meditation and I don't feel sleepy," and you see the result. You have to make a suggestion to yourself. Very easy, yes, "I am not sleepy anymore." Because the body is so easily changed. You know, like you come from Europe to here, you have the time difference. For one day it must be perhaps a problem. But not for a week.

"Ah, jet lag!"

"But when did you come? Third? Today is the tenth!"

"I came on the third."

"And you are still sleepy! Mama mia! It should be only one day."

Abhyasi: Is it very important to do the morning meditation one hour earlier or later?

Master: One hour earlier or later than what?

Abhyasi: Two o'clock or seven o'clock or five o'clock. In this Tai chi meditation...

Master: You should never mix up Chinese and Japanese and Indian meditation. You see, according to the Chinese astrology, I am in the year of monkey or year of the pig, you know, very uncomplimentary! But in English astrology, I am a lion. In Indian astrology, I am a Taurus. Now what am I? I am me—finished! I don't know, maybe my heart is a lion, my stomach is like a boar, and my head is like an ass! Who knows? But why you cut and divide the man into these? We are here.

Abhyasi: But why certain hours of the day?

Master: Stick to the same time. Fix a time and stick to it. You know for me meditation is so easy! I will tell you a funny thing; Verena, she came to Madras and she wanted to make some photographs. She made when I was here, there, and then she said " I want to take one upstairs. It is a nice place." So I went. She said, "Could you sit as if you are meditating?" So I started meditating you see, and I went into the inner condition. Then suddenly I heard some noise, and I opened my eyes. I said, "Have you taken the picture?" She said, "But Chari, it's twenty-five minutes!" No control, you see; you are not supposed to control meditation. I cannot pretend to be meditating; either I meditate or I don't meditate. So now if I just close my eyes, I go in, you see. You can see in my eyes, I look like sleeping.

Very often, when I sit in these meetings, Sahaj Marg meetings, and people are talking, I go into meditation and I cannot keep my eyes open. And then some girl comes and says, "Oh Chari! You are very sleepy." I get a bad name. But I am not sleepy. Because with one part of me, I am trying to concentrate. The concentration makes me go into meditation.

Same thing happens to music. I used to go to lot of music performances. I stopped fifteen years ago. Because I go with my wife and I am sitting in the music hall, full, and the moment I start listening to the music, you know, and my wife says, "Wake up, people know me, what will they think?" But I am not sleeping. So I asked Master. He said, "You know when you meditate properly, you reach a stage of concentration; now when you concentrate you go into meditation—the reverse.

That is why we are not able to read books any more, you see. Because when you read with concentration, the mind goes inside and the book is gone and people think you are sleeping. But it is not sleep, you follow? So the reversibility, you see. Similarly, when I sit and talk to people, hear these people talking, I go like that, you see; I try hard to keep my eyes open. Very often, when I just want to sit in meditation and escape, "Crazy world, what am I doing here?" I don't know, sometimes—it looks so stupid, I am not joking—sometimes I feel so horrible you know, and I feel so angry with Babuji. Literally... (p.199-201)

— ❖ —

"Do you do meditation?"

"Well yes, once or twice a week."

"How long?"

"Oh, sometimes ten minutes, fifteen minutes."

"Fine."

How can you progress? Isn't it? If you have an important meeting or your car is breaking down, you are going to walk for four hours and you go to the car man and buy a new battery, you do everything. If you have to go for a holiday for the weekend, you take four hours to prepare everything, you see. Cut the sandwiches, bake the bread; buy something to take with you; prepare the hamper; put the children to sleep early; start at four o'clock in the morning to avoid the morning car rush out of the city. Now, where do you find the time for all that? But for meditation we have no time. So it is not the fault of the Master, it is not the fault of the system; the fault is always that of the abhyasi.

(p.204-205)

Role of the Master in Human Evolution

Shri P. Rajagopalachari

Many people ask, especially new abhyasis, "Why is there a need for a group satsangh?" He offered three reasons. The first was that when we all sit down and meditate together, the effort is magnified, and is much more than the sum of individual effort.

(p.109)

— ❖ —

We are frequently being asked, "Can I worship Christ and meditate? Can I worship Buddha and meditate?" We must understand that these are like staircases in one building, you see. And it is like saying this *escalier* is Hindu, this *escalier* is Buddhist, that is Christian. That is why Master used to say, "Religions are the kindergarten schools for human beings." They give us some idea of what God is and try to instill in us basic ethical and moral values, nothing more than that. I don't think any religion has ever succeeded in really linking man with God. If you study the history of religions, the founders of the religions got what they got by meditation—whether it was Christ or Buddha. They achieved what they achieved, and in all of them it was by meditation. This is what the respective traditions say, it is not something we say Christ went up on the mountain and meditated for forty days, we are tempted by the Devil, things like that, you see; Buddha meditating under the bodhi tree, again for forty days or forty-one days. So as I was telling some of our Italian abhyasis yesterday, Christ, to my knowledge, was not a Christian, but his teachings became Christianity. He achieved his link with God by direct communion with the Ultimate, through meditation. The same thing for Buddha and Buddhism. Before Buddha there was no Buddhism. Buddha was not a Buddhist.

(p.110-111)

— ❖ —

Satsangh does not mean sitting together, because even one person can be in satsangh. In Sanskrit *sat* means the truth, and He is the truth. God is the truth. That's what Christ meant when he said, "I am the way and the light and the truth." And *sangha* means, 'to be together with.' So satsangh means 'to be associated with the truth.' So whenever we meditate, even alone, it is satsangh. And when five hundred people sit or ten thousand people sit, it can be satsangh, only when each one of us is in touch with the truth, the reality of the Ultimate.

So if you are just sitting with eyes closed and thinking of baguette and honey, it is not satsangh. Others may think it is satsangh. I say this because there are other groups under other traditions singing together, dancing together, things like that, you see. And this was a warning given to me long ago by Master—that they cannot be satsangh. Because that which makes a satsangh a satsangh is missing. So remember this, that in a satsangh the contact with the Ultimate must be maintained, if it is to be a satsangh, and if you are to benefit by that satsangh.

Because each time we sit in satsangh and establish that contact by His grace, we achieve several abilities, capacities. We are able to establish the contact sooner and sooner, and the contact also becomes stronger and stronger, until one day it becomes a permanent contact of the strongest type.

This is why we have to meditate every day, until that act of meditation becomes so perfect that, as Master once told me, "If a man sits and becomes able to plunge into that perfect meditation, he cannot come out of it." So that is meditation, real meditation. Because it is like, you know, you walk through a door, and you are inside the house. Suppose you have a system which says you must walk through this door a hundred and one times before you enter into the house. Is it possible? So you step in, step out, step in, step out, a hundred and one times, you count it, it is ridiculous, you see. But why don't we succeed on the first occasion? Because we have lost the ability to regulate our minds. And this we all know.

That is why Babuji used to say when He was asked, "Why do you ask for meditation for one hour?" He said, "In the beginning, when we start meditation, it is possible that you may not be able to really meditate, even for one minute in that one hour." And progressively we are able to meditate, really meditate, for longer and longer times. Because when we start, much time is wasted in adjusting ourselves to the situation, trying to gain control over our own minds, putting it on the object of meditation and keeping it there. You know, if you have seen old movies where we had carts drawn by horses or bullocks, the man had to bring the cart out of the shed, go and rope the horses one by one, yoke them to the cart and then start driving. This is our situation. First we have to make the body comfortable, and very often you will find that people are not able to do that even during the whole period of meditation. They are twisting and turning and trying to find a comfortable position. After that, we have to start marshaling the forces of the mind, the senses. So if you think over these things, you will really appreciate that to meditate properly takes a great deal of time. And it is only from the time that we really start meditating that our progress begins.

So that is the problem with meditation, that while it holds out an enormous promise, it depends on us, how we do it. And therefore the Master said, "Meditate every day." Because by doing it again and again, we progressively increase our ability to take command of the situation. So the practice becomes very important, you see. It is not only His teachings, it is His practice. So meditate every day, and He has clarified it must be at the same time, in the same place, because then the mind automatically becomes attuned to what it has to do. So it is advisable to have these practices ordered and in a regulated manner. Because then we automatically slip into meditation at the right time. You know, when cows are being milked with machines, electrical machines, if they are not milked at the right time, the milk starts dropping automatically. See, that is the value of regularity. And the British used to say, they used to insist, that people come to work shaven, clean shaven, you see. And you know the reason? Because the act of shaving prepares you for the action of working. Because the first thing a lazy man abandons is shaving. He says, you know, he does something like this (he rubs his cheek) and says, "Okay, I think I'll shave tomorrow."

So you see these are rituals intended to put us into the right frame of mind for that which we have to do. So having the same place, the same time saves us a great deal of preliminary time in sitting down and starting meditation immediately. So, to that extent, they are for our speedier progress. (p.117-120)

— ❖ —

Now, if it is the Centre, such a problem cannot arise. For example, it's like the sun which is the centre of our solar system. It radiates its light and heat; it has no love or hate; it has no favoritism; it has no friends and enemies, it radiates, because that is its function. We can say it is its existence. By its existence it makes the solar system illuminated, and also heats up everything, let us say, by that fact. Now all that is necessary for us to receive its benefits is to present ourselves before it. We don't have to ask, we don't have to pray, we don't have to beg. We only have to expose ourselves. That is what we do in meditation. We imagine that there is a Divine being who has come from the Centre as the Master, and we present ourselves before Him. The Divine has descended in a human form, as the Master. That is all that is necessary. (p.148-149)

— ❖ —

Now, what is the force of gravitation that we have to use to sort of canalize this love, to make ourselves into suns? It is regulation of the mind. Instead of allowing it to sort of fizzle out in unnecessary activities, in multifarious channels... this is the discipline that we follow in raja yoga, essentially in Sahaj Marg. That is why in yogic literature we find the example of the tortoise, which pulls in all its limbs into itself. Sometimes this has been misinterpreted as signifying ascetic practices; but where ascetic practices are enforced by an external discipline, it fails, because the mind does not co-operate. It is almost impossible to have the mind in one direction and the physical tendencies in another direction. And recognizing the fact that the mind is what originates physical activity, raja yoga guides the mental tendencies into one stream, and that is the object of meditation. (p.160)

— ❖ —

Abhyasi: In some of his books Master refers to meditation on the form of the Master and how beneficial it is. As we are told to meditate on Divine light in the heart, this leads to confusion sometimes...?

Chariji: Master has written in his books it was for himself alone, if I remember right. And subsequently he has clarified in many places that we should follow the practice prescribed. And the prescribed practice is meditation on light in the heart. Subsequently he also clarifies that when the devotion for the Master is so great that the form of the Master appears in the heart, then it is the right time to meditate on the form of the Master. If we start meditating on the form before the form appears itself, by itself, naturally, then it becomes artificial. What it really means is that the Master must become the light of our life, then we find Him instead of the light; then is the appropriate time.

The second thing is, when the form appears we must meditate on the full form, not just on the face. That is from the foot up to the top of the head, everything must be there. Now when it is artificial, and people take the form of the Master for meditation, they take only the face. For the Master, Babuji, it was possible, because the moment he saw Him, he developed a hundred percent devotion for Him. Therefore, he could start to do meditation on the form of his Master. It doesn't apply for all of us.

Then once I discussed with Master, there is a third stage. And that is when the form also disappears from the heart. And I think we come to the stage which Master calls light without luminosity. So we have the first stage which is light in the heart, when people sometimes see the light itself as a luminous thing. As we advance, it becomes light without any features, just the idea of light is there. So in the first stage we have a sort of refinement from the grosser light to the subtle light. Then the idea of devotion brings the Master into the heart. And for most, if not all abhyasis it stops with that. I mean the idea of the Master in the heart, the presence of the Master goes on and on you see. The third stage, when the form also disappears, there is nothing in the heart, no light, no form, nothing. That I think is a very difficult and very rare condition. It is also very difficult, because to have to meditate on nothing or nothingness is almost impossible. The other difficulty is we become attached in an emotional way to the form of the Master, and we are not willing to give it up. I think the third stage is possible only when we can love the Master without loving his form itself. I would suggest that is the requirement of all love; that the love of the form is transferred to the love of the essence which has no form. (p.175-176)

The Fruit of the Tree
Shri P. Rajagopalachari

I may perhaps also tell you the importance of doing the meditation at the right time. Since we have talked about the cleaning, we might as well talk of the meditation. Because the cleaning prepares the system in one way, the meditation fulfills our spiritual requirements in another way. The whole problem comes because some people say, "Well I cannot meditate at such and such time, can I do it later?" So we say, well, you are not able to do the cleaning in the evening because you come at nine o'clock, then you're too tired to do the meditation, combine both before you go to bed. But this is an exception for one or two occasions when you're really tired, but people begin to adopt it as a continuous thing all the year round because it suits them. I have never found that any serious abhyasi had any problem about doing the meditation at the specified time or the cleaning at the specified time. So it only means that until our interest in our own spiritual development is established, we have these problems.

(p.10-11)

— ❖ —

You see, we are sometimes astonished that people who have been meditating for so many years suddenly become wild, in a very real sense. I am not criticizing, but it happens. Suddenly they become wild, and lack direction, lack self-control, and they go wrong in such a way that no ordinary human being can go wrong. I used to wonder why. Then one day I discovered, or rather it was revealed to me in my meditation, that our sadhana has two aspects to it. The development or the acquisition of our regulatory ability over our mind and the thing which we forget, you see, the heart. Now Babuji was, perhaps, as usual, you know, very shy of emphasizing the need, in an abhyasi, to love the Master. He never liked to say these things. But he gives a hint: that constant remembrance is superior to meditation. It has been mentioned in his books, he has spoken about it so many times, that when we are able to establish constant remembrance, the need for meditation drops off. And when love for the person remembered develops, constant remembrance need no longer exist. Because as long as we are practising, or trying to practise constant remembrance, it is a conscious activity. But when love has come, you don't need to think every few minutes and ask yourself whether you love or not.

So meditation is important; before meditation the discipline is important; that is, that we do it at the right time, in the right ways. When we are able to do it correctly, constant remembrance becomes possible. (p.14)

— ❖ —

So what do you do when you sit in meditation? You direct your attention, like I focus the torch on the object, it is still in my hand, I can put it this way, I can put it this way, I can put it this way; also up, and see a plane perhaps. So this direction of the beam of light, from my hand to the object, is the attention, the focus. Similarly I focus my attention on the heart, on the light in the heart, during meditation. Now in some way, there is a movement within me, by Master's grace, if it happens; everybody doesn't move—sometimes it takes fifteen years to move. (p.52)

— ❖ —

All that we see during meditation is the release of our samskara. It's like a record playing music. Whatever it is, it comes. You know, if you are cooking potatoes and you stir the pot, you get the smell of potatoes. So we have samskaras here, and when you are meditating it is released and it comes in contact with the mind, so you get the same impression which made the samskaras first. It is not really important, it only shows that something is coming out. A common example, you know, like a child when it eats something and vomits, it can only bring out what it has eaten, it cannot create something and bring it out.

So nothing can come which has not been inside. That is why we say, don't give importance to these things. (p.56)

— ❖ —

People come and they meditate for six months, then they say, "My wife does not like meditation," and they stop; or a wife says, "My husband does not like meditation"—they stop. You must be willing to accept that change can come only if you totally reject your present circumstance. Then you can have like that [he snaps his fingers]—change. (p.60)

— ❖ —

...we must know, not where the heart is, but how to listen to it.

It's like a telephone. I can telephone you from wherever I am, but you need not know where I am. All that you need is to listen to me. Isn't it? Why does it matter where I am? What I say will be the same whether I am in Timbuktu or in Toronto. It's not going to make a difference. So the location of the heart is not important. What it says is important. But that we never hear. In meditation we try to attend to the heart and then slowly it begins to speak, that's what you call the conscience, and the more you listen, the more loud it becomes, powerful it becomes. Then you get the guidance from inside—now you want guidance from outside. (p.66)

— ❖ —

We never perceive light in the heart. Well, Master says it is a mere suggestion. I mean it is there in the beginner's pamphlet. Imagine that there is light in the heart. He does not say see the light. Because the whole exercise is to bring in the light. It is like a man who is in a dark room with the curtains drawn and wants light before he'll open the curtains. The curtains have to be opened and then the light streams in by itself.

Master's instructions are very clear: imagine that there is light in the heart, illuminating it from inside, and meditate on that. Do not try to see, or project light. The instruction is very clear. All that you have to do in answering the question is to show that bit of instruction to the abhyasi and say, "This is it."

Incidentally, there I had once a very illuminating experience. You know I was also bothered, because in Hindu tradition, they talk of the Divine presence like something which has the brilliance of a million suns, which makes your eyes, you know, become glazed. That sort of thing. And I never saw the light. Every time I sat in meditation, I went deeper and deeper, I plunged sometimes into *samadhi*. I lost body consciousness, occasionally fell down, but never saw the light. And when I asked Babuji, he said that that is the problem, you see, we never see the light, because light is not our goal.

But on one side you have these promises of yogic literature, religious literature; on the other side you have the old man, my Master, "Meditate on a light which you are never going to see." And on the third corner of the triangle is our occult literature which says that on which you meditate, that you shall become. Now this Mission, and this method seemed to fulfill none of these promises. And one day I was sitting in my garden outside, it was dark, about eight p.m. Suddenly I saw a bright point of light moving fast, from the western horizon up. It remained bright for about, say thirty degrees above, and suddenly vanished. Then I remembered, or I understood, it was one of these modern contraptions—satellites. It had been low enough on the horizon to reflect light. When it came into the earth's shadow it blinked out. Then I understood that what I am seeing as the dark sky is full of light. But you never see light unless there is an object there. (p.133-134)

— ❖ —

Q: Should all of the Centres now begin having men and women sit separately for group meditation?

A: As a policy, it would be nice to try it. I mean, there is no harm in it. After all, you are going to meditate for half an hour, and assuming that you don't propose to "mooch" when everybody has their eyes closed, [laughter] what is the harm in sitting separately? I mean, I am asking a blunt question. One would hardly imagine that a meditation group is where something is going on when everybody has his eyes closed, and is hopefully meditating. This is the first place where we should try it, because this is the place where our freedom is going to be interfered least with. Isn't it? I mean, it seems to be logical to me. This is the one place where we don't propose to do anything at all, and therefore it doesn't matter where we sit. So why not you all kindly extend that little co-operation and try it out?

There is nothing artificial about it, nothing unnatural about it. And I assure you, if you try it out you will feel the benefits yourself, in so many ways. You know I have come across—I mean, you will excuse my mentioning this, it's not a very palatable thing—but I have come across meetings of this sort where because the sexes have been mixed in accommodations, quarters, there have been avoidable incidents. And the only provocation was proximity. The person who approached wasn't intending to do it. But you find yourself alone with somebody, and there is the good old Adam you know, waking up; and you can't blame Adam. Adam **did** fall, so Adam continues to fall.

So why I am saying this is, if we from the beginning have a healthy policy that, you know, opportunity will not be given for accidents of this nature to happen, we are much better off from the beginning. The minimum benefit is it saves embarrassment to all concerned, and it could possibly save problems. And this is not something new, it has happened in many places, on many occasions.

So it's a very healthy thing, even in accommodation, unless husband and wife and kids want to stay together for obvious reasons—okay. But let me warn my sisters especially, you see, that they are the vulnerable element, and it's for their sake that we are proposing these changes, you see, and there is no harm in this. (p.166-167)

— ❖ —

Q: I'm a little confused about the separating of the sexes.

A: Don't worry. Do it.

Q: No. But I want to just ask you something. If we're all the same inside, why would the energy be different between the females and the males during the sitting?

A: We are not all the same, only the souls are the same, we are not the same yet.

Q: Well, if all the souls are the same...

A: It's like saying all the brains are the same. You know, all the brains are the same, physiologically.

Q: Yeah, but I thought that in Sahaj Marg we are all...

A: No, no, no. You are misusing Sahaj Marg to claim an equality for a wrong purpose. Claim it for a right purpose. What is so hot about being separated for half an hour, that you people want to protest about it so much? What's wrong with it? (p.172)

— ❖ —

Q: Is it common to have a bout of severe headache, anger, intense sleepiness, immediately after meditation?

A: It's not common, but it can happen sometimes. There can be sleepiness if you go very deep into meditation. I used to have this problem and I wrote to Babuji about it. I wrote to Him, and he answered back, that as activity is the life of the body, some sort of inaction is the life of the soul. Therefore when we go deep into meditation, the life of the soul takes over. And so we want to be inactive, and therefore, we like to lie down and sleep, and things like that.

I also have had for many years severe headache after meditation. The deeper the meditation, the stronger the headache. And it still happens sometimes. This also I referred to my Master. He advised me to stop meditation for some time. But it didn't work, so I continued to meditate. If the headache comes, we put up with it.

Anger also comes sometimes because of the same reason as the sleepiness, or lethargy. Because following on a good meditation, we wish to relax and be quiet, and when our friends, relations they come and disturb us, we get annoyed. So they are all three in a sense related: anger, sleepiness, headache, they are all in a sense related to the same cause. But we should not be bothered by them. (p.186)

— ❖ —

Q: For many months, my meditation has been changing timewise. Frequently I find it extends well over the hour, even to two hours. When I come out of it I know it was not sleep and it seems like only a short time has passed. What does this mean?

A: Babuji has said, that as far as possible, we should not meditate for more than one hour at a time. So we have to exercise some sort of discriminatory control over our meditation time. It can happen occasionally that we meditate for more. But if it is a regular affair, then we should perhaps keep an alarm clock and get out of it. Because in Sahaj Marg too much meditation puts a pressure on the brain—at one sitting. Because Babuji has said we can meditate for one hour at a time, as many times as you have time for in the day, but no more than one hour at a time.

It is quite possible for a one hour sitting to look as if it lasted five minutes, and for a five minutes sitting to look as if it was one hour. It has nothing to do with the quality of the transmission. It only shows that there is a change in our perception of temporality as we understand it. It is good to meditate between two and four a.m. because Babuji has said that's the best time during the twenty-four hours. (p.190)

Q: It seems sometimes in meditation that I feel intense emotion, that I want to cry, and I feel depressed. What could be the reason for this, and what should I do?

A: Emotion generally comes only during the beginning of an abhyasi's life. It's very common that in the first year or the second year of our abhyas, there are very often intense emotional bouts. Babuji told me that it is because of the gratitude towards the Master, at the inner level of existence, and it is not a conscious thing, and therefore the heart expresses it in the only way it can, by tears.

But if it continues into our abhyas later on, it is not a desirable thing. Emotion is not desirable for spiritual life. Babuji distinguishes very clearly between emotions and feelings. Feelings are essential. Emotions are likely to damage our spiritual growth. Often it becomes a habit, emotion becomes a habit, and that should be avoided. That's all. (p.191)

— ❖ —

Q: Can we meditate on Master's form, even if we have not seen the Master when he was alive?

A: Meditation on the Master's form is supposed to begin only when the form appears spontaneously before us, and it must be natural. If you try to force the form upon yourself for meditation, it is unnatural.

Of course, Babuji started meditating on his Master's form from day one. But he has also written that it was for him alone. For others, like us, we have to wait till our devotion to the Master is so much, our love for him is so much, that when we look for the light in the heart, we see him there. As for the second part, Master himself has written that you cannot meditate on one whom you have not been—what shall we say—with, in the physical existence. And the need for a living Master is emphasized in *Voice Real*.

Q: I have felt during meditation that my bonds with my children have been severed, and that was acceptable to me. But then later, I felt that the bonds with my Master were severed, and I thought how could that be?

A: Perhaps they are just projections of your mind. Of course, it is possible that one's connection with the Master can be severed. But it is important to remember that the Master never cuts it. The abhyasi can cut it, and that is His benediction, you see.

(p.192-193)

— ❖ —

Now it is the mercy of the Master that He leaves such a light in our hearts. In the days of the gas burning water boilers in bathrooms, you have seen there used to be a tiny pilot flame, which would light up when needed. But it never went out. That is what we have in our hearts—a spark of Divinity which is eternally there, and as I suggested yesterday, that is this atomic piece of Divinity that is in all of us. And that is what we try to fan into a big flame and a conflagration by our meditation. (p.211)

Heart to Heart, Volume I
Shri P. Rajagopalachari

So you see how we can convert an ordinary, mundane thing like drinking coffee into an experience, or a smoke into an experience, and then to boost our ego into saying, "Yes, you are right, we put more and more money on that experience to prove to ourselves that it's a valuable experience." So instead of accepting the reality of an experience, we are loading what we suppose to be an experience, with all the unreality that we can possibly load onto it, and present it as something novel, something unique, something wonderful. This tendency we should not sort of import into our meditative states, because the whole idea of meditation is to perceive reality, to become one with the reality that we perceive; finally, to merge into that reality ourselves, so that our separate identity no longer exists. (p.94)

— ❖ —

Therefore, spirituality says, "Die before you die, and you shall see what is the glory of Death itself, what it opens out beyond into: the eternal life that is promised." It only means doing what the runner is doing, you see: that you run until you are almost collapsing, and then you find the miraculous awakening of fresh powers inside yourself, **from** inside yourself, of which you could never have dreamt, because you never exerted yourself to that level before. Spirituality says, "That is the outer world; here you do it inside." Close your eyes, meditate, and the feeling comes that I'm diving deep into some sort of a bottomless hole, very dark. And then the tendency, sometimes the need, is to open one's eyes to reassure oneself that one is still in this world of human beings. That is the danger.

It is like the runner stopping at the fifteenth mile to see "Oh, do I have that hidden resource that Chari was talking about?" You can't feel it. It's gone, you see. It's like, you know, the petrol tank. Sometimes we used to have—I don't know whether you still have—an emergency small tank which you opened up when the main tank went dry. Some drivers were careless; they left it open all the time. So when it stopped, it stopped finally, because the reserve petrol was always open. The idea of a reserve tank is the capacity should be reserved for those emergent occasions when there is no gas station nearby. Then you open it and move to the nearest place. But if you are leaving it open all the time, you have lost the capacity to have control over it, which is what we are doing with our physical energies: draining them to the last possible drop of essence and then, when the need for a reserve comes, it just isn't there.

So the sensible human way of living is not to drain your reserve capacities unnecessarily. In any field...

So, you see, when we go into meditation, we learn all these things: that I have to die in my meditation to be reborn in that meditation, and to come out yet the same Paul, the same Bill, the same whatever you are, you see. But with a very, very different outlook on life; with a very, very different inside that has now been opened, changed, cleaned up, refurbished in some mysterious way. Therefore, every time we sit in meditation and we go deep into it, we come out new—renewed, you can say. That is why meditation is refreshing. That is why meditation is never exhausting, you know, however deep you go into it you come out fresh. Pains are gone, aches are gone, more of the heart—which is a very great need. There is solace derived from ourselves, from within ourselves, by ourselves. So we see that, in a very real sense, we are becoming independent of the universe. We seek no solace outside, we get it from inside. Others take renewal from outside, we get it from inside. The others take renewed strength from outside, we get it from inside. Then we find the ultimate experience, that within **me** is the universe. Not this which I see outside, however vast it might be: ten million, ten billion light-years big, so what? It is only a parody of what is inside. This has no limit that can be measured in terms of light-years. You cannot measure this at all; it is **truly** infinite.

(p.100-101)

— ❖ —

We are always afraid of death. That's a very natural fear. But to be told that perhaps, my dear friend, you don't exist—even now—would be awful, wouldn't it? But when you plunge into yourself in meditation and, if, by Master's grace, by the solemnity of your experience, you are able to experience those spiritual states where you find first nothing, then you find yourself all alone, and then you find that the universe into which you are put all alone by yourself is really you...!

The universe is you. You are there as something experiencing yourself in a cosmic form. Then comes this, you know, really brilliant, fascinating experience that "I am the Universe." (p.102)

...Babuji has said, written perhaps in *Voice Real*, that, you know, there are three ways of meditating. One when we sit as abhyasis and meditate on the light in the heart. The second is the higher stage when we think, I mean when we sit in meditation, and meditate on the form of the Master, the form of the Master in the heart. There is a third stage about which not much is said in our literature. Perhaps someday I shall reveal it! [laughter]

Q: How about today?

A: How about today? Okay! [laughter] It is when the Master begins to meditate on the abhyasi. And that is a very rare occurrence. You see, such a person should be born, and such a Master should be—I mean it is not blasphemous to say this—such a Master is blessed when he gets a disciple upon whom He has to meditate! (p.122-123)

— ❖ —

What about the thoughts that are bothering us when we are meditating? They are the most troublesome interrupters of our meditating process. And what about our attention during meditation? Essentially, it is this attention you know, if you put it in the right place: in the heart, on the divine light in the heart, nothing is going to bother us. It's a well-known fact that if you are absorbed in a good book, nothing disturbs you. You start reading at three in the afternoon, and, after going through it in a very highly absorbed condition, you find it is dark, it has become nine o'clock, and you have been reading all the time without any interruption. Now how is that possible?

I, you know, occasionally open my eyes during meditation to see what's going on, for one reason: occasionally, a new abhyasi can be overpowered by transmission and fall backwards or forwards. So for this reason, we keep a watch. Yesterday, it so happened that just as I opened my eyes—it's a brief exposure, you know, we don't go on looking, just a momentary flash—I heard a baby or a child crying there. And instantly the mother got up from here and rushed out. Now, that was very good for the mother; better, even, for the child; but not so good for the abhyasi who was the mother. Because she was not really meditating. Her attention was centred on the child there while sitting with her eyes closed here.

So you see, these are the problems of meditation. We have children. Why only beeping watches? Somebody may be thinking of the potential fire in his house. And another typically North American habit, because you have this wonderful telephone system, you keep calling home every third minute or fifth minute, "How are the kids? How is the cat? How is the dog?" and then agonizing over what you hear, when they tell you, "Poor Jill is sick." And Jill may be a cat for all we know. So, I'm not saying that we shouldn't love our cats and dogs, and our kids, but this is a serious business, you know. We are expected to give up the world and life itself to achieve the spiritual goal. So, starting from the beeps of the watch to the kids at home, we should not allow any of them to interfere with us.

Now, all that I am saying is I have two or three channels in my mind: one, concern for the children at home; one, concern for my meditation; one, for my neighbour's watch. I have three channels in the mind—I mean a **minimum** of three channels in the mind. How effective can my meditation be? Because the effort during meditation is to bring all the powers of the mind into one channel. But we are sitting with three different dish antennae pointing in three different directions. So it is not at all a surprise that we are not able to meditate properly and, therefore, are not making progress. (p.183-184)

— ❖ —

Q: When employment is seven a.m. to three p.m. one day, three p.m. to eleven the next, and eleven p.m. to seven a.m. the next day, how do we meditate, and clean, and pray before bedtime? Thank you.

A: Well, this is only a small thing, you know. There are people who are in jobs where they don't know when they are working, and when they are going to be off—like a pilot in a plane, for instance. Yet we find time to eat, to sleep—all the functions of existence—because we consider them necessary. If you consider, also, meditation to be necessary as a daily part of your existence, you would very easily find the time for it. (p.186-187)

— ❖ —

There is a famous Upanishad, you see, which teaches of a disciple, young fellow, who goes to the Master and in the Eastern tradition they don't teach—they allow you to learn. The Master tells him, "Go and sit and meditate and come back." This man meditates for ten, twelve years, and in his meditation it appears to him that food is the ultimate thing. Because by food everything lives, through food everything exists; all are searching for food, it is food which is the problem: to earn it we have to work. So he comes to the Master and says, "Food is the ultimate thing." The Master smiles blissfully, you see, this boy is on the first step towards knowledge. He says, "Yes, my son, but there is something beyond it, go back and meditate again." And this son of his goes into the jungle, starts meditating again, after a further twelve years, he says, "What is the use of food if I don't breathe! Food exists in abundance. If I stop breathing what is the good of all the food?" So he says, "I have found it. Eureka!" He comes back to the Master. "Master, breath is the ultimate." The Master is blissful, he says, "Yes, my son, wonderful discovery, but yet there is something beyond." So third period of meditation, twelve years more. He comes back and says, "The mind, without the mind what can exist? It is the mind which tells me where is food, what is food, how to get there." Master is again very pleased. He says, "Yes, you have made the third grade, now go back again." Then he comes back with the discovery, "It is knowledge. What is the use of a mind if there is no knowledge, if it is deranged?" He says, "Knowledge." The guru says, "Wonderful. Go again and do it." Ultimately he comes back with the final answer, up to which he has evolved, he says, "It is bliss. Because, if I have food, if I am able to breathe, if I have the mind, if I have all the knowledge, but if I have no bliss of existence, what on earth is this existence useful for?" Isn't it? There the Upanishad unfortunately stops.

But my Master, our Master, Babuji Maharaj, went beyond. He said, "What is beyond peace? What is beyond bliss? There must be something. There cannot be an end in an endless universe. Look for that." Therefore, Sahaj Marg takes up from where the Upanishads left off, the Vedas left off, and goes beyond.

(p.202-204)

— ❖ —

Don't estimate your prowess by the things that you have produced on canvas, or in buildings of stone and steel, or even art in marble. Go inside, go to the roots of yourself, roots of your existence and see from there where this flowering is going to happen at the end. Therefore, we meditate on the inner self, in the heart, which is the core of being, the core of existence. In the heart, the core of the heart itself, which is that Divine spark of Divine light, which we are supposed to imagine as the object of our meditation. (p.209)

— ❖ —

"Oh, I planted this seed twenty days ago, it is not yet germinating, let me dig it up and see what's happening to the seed." We destroy it. We have to put it in, water it and go on watering it until something appears, and wait. That is why in spirituality, Babuji used to say, "Think that the Divine light is in the heart, try to hold this thought and wait." Somebody once asked him, you know, a very illiterate sort of person asked Babuji, "What exactly is meditation?" He gave a beautiful answer. He said, "Suppose you invite me to dinner tonight at your house, what would you do?" He said, "Master, I would clean the house first, see that everything is shipshape, then my wife would prepare the food, the best that we can possibly offer, then we would make up the place where you are going to eat, lay the plates, or the leaves, and await your coming." He said, "The same thing in meditation—clean your heart, purify it, have everything ready and wait for the appearance of the Master." (p.215)

— ❖ —

What is meditation? Because I find now new people are coming. Today I had a peculiar experience that during the meditation, which was utterly still, I seemed to hear some people muttering something, possibly doing some prayers. It is possible to hear, when you are totally still, what is going on in another person's mind. Babuji calls it reading. I have often found this: that some abhyasis, even when they meditate they cannot give up the former practices of chanting. Some do the Hindu chanting, prayers, mantras; some do the Christian. So when we meditate, if you clutter up the mind with another activity like thinking of a japa, or a mantra, or whatever it is, now there are two things struggling and neither will succeed. Because with one part of your mind you are trying to introduce stillness by meditation. With another part of the mind, you are trying to create an activity of thought, a stream of thought. Naturally, they are opposing each other. Also the fundamental law that the mind should be one—if you divide it into two the power of the mind is split into two streams—comes into operation. Therefore, we fail in both activities. Neither the mantra becomes useful, nor does the meditation become useful.

So I want to advise, especially my Indian brothers and sisters who are here, that if they want to take to Sahaj Marg meditation they should take to it completely, fully, to the exclusion of everything else. We cannot have two gods; we cannot have two methods; we cannot have two concurrent currents in the mind. So that is something, because perhaps I was able to be still, I could hear the voices here and there. You see, there were a couple of them.

So when we meditate, we should only meditate. What should we meditate upon? The light in the heart. That is the second problem, you see. Because we find Christians wanting to meditate on Christ, Buddhists on Buddha, perhaps Sikhs on Guru Govind Singh or Nanak, I don't know. But then, you see, you cannot accept two systems again. It is like trying to create vegetarian beef. It's not possible. Or beefy brinjals. (p.289-290)

— ❖ —

Now if in this process we keep introducing other created things, whether gods, mantras, what have you, we are again going backwards. It's like pressing the car's accelerator with one foot and the brake with the other. Fortunately, no car has yet been designed in which this mistake can happen. Because both are operated by the same foot. But suppose, perversely, somebody, you know, takes off the leg from the other pedal and tries—you will only damage the car. So what happens when we try to meditate with two systems, or two gurus, or two different warring things in our mind? Even if one is good in itself, we are damaging ourselves.

Therefore, please bear in mind, meditation only according to the system—whichever system you adopt. We have no quarrels with that. You want to go to tai chi, for heaven's sake do it. But do tai chi alone. You want to do Islamic meditation, do only that. You want to do that given by Nanak, do only that. Don't mix two things. Because each may be good, but the mixture may be disastrous. Fire is good, explosives are good; the mixture is disastrous. Isn't it? Except when necessary.

So that is the second thing. In stilling the mind we should not introduce other things. In meditation we should not forget that we are going from complexity to simplicity and start off with a little bit of this, a little bit of that, little bit of that Christ for ten minutes, Buddha for ten minutes, Confucius for ten minutes, Krishna for ten minutes, and finally Master for ten minutes. Some people are doing it, even today. Which only means we are cluttering up the whole thing with again a five-part complexity, four-part complexity, three-part complexity. So no mantras, please; no second object of meditation, please. (p.291-293)

So we are afraid to delve into the self, you know. I know a person, a classic example, who wanted to start meditation, but he couldn't close his eyes and look in. He would sit for a moment, and then come screaming out of it, and rush to hold tight to somebody nearby, the preceptor. It's not easy to meditate. I mean, to even start meditation. I sincerely believe it shows that we have already reached a certain high level of evolution—where we are able to even contemplate this horrible experiment of looking into ourselves. What are you going to find inside, you see? (p.296)

— ❖ —

Therefore, this awesome business of looking into the self is avoided by most people. They say, "What on earth should we meditate for?" (p.297)

— ❖ —

Therefore, fear has to be overcome, and that first manifestation of fear is in the inability to meditate. Fear of closing the eyes, looking into the self—that has to go. (p.298)

Heart to Heart, Volume II
Shri P. Rajagopalachari

Therefore philosophy says: if you follow my way, it is easier, quicker, simpler; whereas if you go out into the vast universe, you are never going to be able to see anything there, because no human being, and not even millions of generations of human beings, are going to have the time sufficient to study the universe completely.

This wisdom guided the Eastern societies to go inwards into philosophical research, which really meant research into yourself, because it would be an absurdity to see God in trees and stones and birds and beautiful things. So, if each human being had to delve inwards, he or she could only delve into himself or herself, and in this way evolved the science of yoga, meditation.

(p.5)

— ❖ —

People may ask, how can we be happy in our meditation? Can meditation give happiness?

We are not happy in our meditation, we are meditating—that's all. Happy or sorry it is because of other circumstances. This is another mistake in your thinking. We meditate. Happiness and sorrow result out of our samskaras in other ways, and not because we meditate.

And now let me take up another point, that we are sitting and doing nothing to help the world. Suppose Babuji had been born in Europe, and he had thought like my friend and did not meditate but became a social worker, visited jails, did poor feeding and was very happy that he was helping people, what would have happened to the world today? It does not apply only to Babuji, it applies to all of us. We are at a higher level of service, whereas those are at a lower level of service. My learned friend must no doubt know the quotation from Confucius that when you give a man a fish, you feed him once; when you teach him to fish, he can feed himself all his life. So, physical help is the lowest level of service; serving people by educating them at the mental level is a higher level of service. The spiritual service is absolutely the highest. So to think that we are sitting meditating and not doing anything to change the world is a foolish thought. We are trying to help humanity at the highest level, leaving the lower levels to those who are capable of that. Now, are you happy?

Now, I would like to add something else to what I was answering to our brother. When a man who is meditating feels that he is not helping humanity, there is something wrong. Can you tell me what is wrong? [laughter] You see, the problem is we have been used to helping people by giving something, by doing something; but in meditation we neither give nor do anything for others. Not directly. This leaves us in a bit of a confusion. And this confusion grows because we don't see the direct effect of our meditating, or changing ourselves. This is the, shall we say, European mind's obsession with cause and effect. The human mind has been trained in the West to do something and see the result immediately. We are not prepared to accept that we can introduce a cause, the effect of which we may never see.

(p.18-20)

— ❖ —

So the exercise to think of Him constantly is what we try to achieve by thinking of Him occasionally in meditation. (p.53)

— ❖ —

..."Satan finds questions for idle minds to ask!" Because when we are fully occupied we have no questions. It's a fact. We all know it. Very often I have found in the time of my Master and now, it is the people who don't meditate who want to know how to meditate. It is the people who don't clean themselves who are worried about blockages, grossness.

So the true answer to our questions is not answers, but doing... (p.62)

— ❖ —

Then they say, "Oh, it is so bad, I am not able to even meditate." It is as if—what shall I say—as tragic, as comic, as a sick man saying, "I am too sick to take medicine." It has got to be done. And very often people come and say, "Oh, you know, I haven't been able to meditate for one year, and I have no results." This is even a bigger contradiction, that we expect results without doing anything. I mean, these are all the experiences of the last two, three days, and it is causing me much, what should I say, sorrow. That abhyasis don't meditate for two years, and then complain that they have no results. When you ask them why they don't meditate, they say they feel blocked: "How did this block come?" "Maybe I did something wrong." "Are you continuing to do it wrong now?" "Yes, unfortunately." [laughter] "Why do you continue to do it?" "Because I am not meditating." [laughter]

You see it goes round and round in circles. So what should we do about these things? After all, we are asked to meditate a maximum of one hour in the morning, fifteen, twenty minutes cleaning in the evening and ten minutes prayer at night. We don't have the time for this. Or we don't have the inclination for it. Even one abhyasi came and told me that every time he wanted to meditate he found something else to do. Now, how is it possible to find something else to do, when you have something to do already? It only means the mind is not on meditation. So the only remedy was to advise him, "Please, do it."

So you see how ridiculous this situation is, that we create all these problems by misunderstanding, by misapplication of the will. Because there is one thing which Babuji always used to emphasize: that if you have the will power to apply at all, to anything, it must be applicable to anything that you want to do. So if you cannot do one thing and can do another thing with the same will power, it only means that you want to do one thing while you don't want to do the other. The will power is not lacking and is not to be blamed.

So you see, essentially the inability to meditate is not really an inability to meditate, but an unwillingness to meditate. Babuji has told so many abhyasis in my presence, he said, "If my meditating for you could benefit, I would do the meditation also for you gladly." But it is as silly as saying, "If I could eat for you, I would eat for you." You must eat. So please try to understand this: that whenever we say we can't meditate, we don't want to meditate. Because there is nothing in nature which can oppose a determined will. And what is necessary is to reassign our priorities, and do the meditation. If you do this, you will find there are no more questions, the path to the goal becomes smooth and progress is assured. (p.64-65)

— ❖ —

And if we come to Sahaj Marg because it's a natural way of development, and here also we fossilize everything by making it a system, a routine, then that big danger comes which Babuji was always expressing, that meditation becomes a mechanical, lifeless thing. Then how will we progress? So while we have to have rules and regulations, they must be like our clothes, loose, comfortable, and which you can throw off when necessary. (p.75-76)

— ❖ —

Now there are occasions like that if you make meditation too much of a regimented thing, people may sit as if they are meditating, but they don't meditate. Now this is something dangerous I am saying today, You should not misunderstand it and say, "Oh, today I don't feel like meditating, I won't meditate." That is not the intention at all. The intention is that instead of making it an unnatural, regimented thing, we must make it so natural, like our breathing for instance, that without meditation we cannot possibly exist. Now, what is the difference? When we obey rules and sit down to meditate—like the first of the ten maxims: awake at dawn and sit for meditation—we obey with the mind, with the intellect. But when we learn to love the Master, and make this part of our life itself, then we put our heart into it. Then it works. So while we must insist of course, very forcibly too, that people must be regular, people must sit at proper times, people, preceptors especially, must also have this charitable attitude to allow a little flexibility. "Okay! Today, instead of coming at eight you have come at nine; all right, I'll give you a sitting," not be like policemen, "No, no, no more today, you see, my time is over." Because we don't know under what circumstances the poor fellow could not meditate. So on one side we have to have discipline, on the other side we have to have flexibility. (p.77-78)

— ❖ —

...Babuji himself has told me several times that he rarely meditated, even when he was an abhyasi under Lalaji. His preceptor was Pandit Rameshwar Prasad whose name appears in *Reality at Dawn*. The book is dedicated to him. And whenever he meditated, he meditated for something like three minutes, five minutes. There were people at his time, Lalaji's disciples, who used to meditate like rishis. Yet he became the Master and they were still abhyasis. So this also shows us that it is not the duration of time that we sit that is important, I mean the duration of meditation. It is what we do with that time that is important. What is the use of sitting for one hour if I am not meditating even three minutes during that one hour? Of course I have obeyed Master's ten maxims, but it is useless. I have obeyed it outwardly, but inwardly I have not obeyed it. (p.78-79)

— ❖ —

Well, we have a place for everything else in our life, you have a toilet; you have a place to brush your teeth in; you have a place in which you keep your combs and your cosmetics. You go to those respective places for the respective functions, and a dining table to sit down and eat on, a bedroom to sleep in. So what is so wonderful about having a place to meditate in. Because it's a funny thing, many people even have told me that they have no place to meditate. I cannot understand how it is possible. You can sit at your dining table and meditate in the chair. You can sit on your bed and meditate in your bedroom. I don't see any difficulty. Unless people nowadays have become so compartmentalized in their heads, that they want a room only for meditation so it must be separately kept. Now Babuji did not say, "Build a separate room for meditation." He said, "Have a place for meditation." We have hundreds of places in our houses. I have known people sitting on staircases when there is no room and they are there able to meditate. People sitting on the floor, people sitting on the roads. So when Babuji is there, and there is such a big rush that there is no place, we can sit on staircases and meditate, on the pavement and meditate. So it is not difficult to meditate there, we need an inducement, that the Master is there, there is no other place, therefore we will sit here. Now, if that is the only place available, and if you really feel in your heart that the Master is always with you, why can't you sit on the staircase every day and meditate? (p.80)

— ❖ —

So we begin with externally imposed discipline and rise progressively until we discipline ourselves from inside ourselves. At the first stage it is artificial, enforced from outside. At the top it is natural, my own way of existence. It is no longer a discipline I obey—I am disciplined. So similarly we must start meditation, cleaning, prayer at night, all these, as impositions on us. Something which has to be done because the Master says it must be done if you want to grow. But as we develop, it is something we do because we want to do it. At the end of our journey it is still there, but now it's all natural.

Then if you ask the Master, "Are you meditating?," he won't be able to answer yes or no, because for him whether he is awake or asleep or dreaming, it is all meditation. (p.81)

— ❖ —

So we must develop into that stage where, if you close your eyes in meditation, what you see within yourself must be so astoundingly wonderful, and pulling you like a magnet towards Himself, that without the Master's grace we can never come out of it again. It is the Self that must put us into *samadhi*. Fortunately for us—I mean, don't be afraid—fortunately for us the Master pulls us out every time. Not because it is necessary for us to be here, it is really not necessary for us to be here, but because

he is the Master of Nature, he does not want to go counter to the laws of Nature. He brings us back again and again to live out the allotted span of time. So that is why even those of us who are able to plunge into the depths of meditation have to come out.
(p.95-96)

— ❖ —

Q: What is the criterion for good or poor meditation, and something which is not an intellectual interpretation or a misleading sensation?

A: There are no such things as a good meditation or a poor meditation. There is only meditation. If it is rightly done, it is effective. Meditation should be effective. Either we meditate or we don't meditate. (p.157)

— ❖ —

Q: Is the condition of being completely 'gone' in a sitting a sign of being one with the Master? How can the inner condition of being one with Him be described?

A: The condition of being 'gone' is only one of absorption in your own inner state. It has nothing to do with being one with the Master. How to describe being one with the Master? Each one has to find out for himself. So when we ask this question, it means we have not come to that condition yet. (p.159)

— ❖ —

So however much we may practise meditation, you know, however seriously, however sincerely, however dedicatedly, the real spiritual benefit will elude us until we give our heart. So as long as we talk of love of the Master saying "my heart" and "your heart," it's not love. (p.175)

— ❖ —

Love is an individual affair. It concerns only the lover and the beloved. Sometimes we see in these talks people say, "Let us give our hearts." I mean this cannot be a mass sacrifice, you know. ... This has to come individually, for each person. ... So each one has to work for this, not a group effort. Group meditation but individual love. (p.177)

— ❖ —

For the last ten days or so, I have been hearing my brother Patrick Fleury saying that meditation is very simple, it is true, but I don't want you to make the mistake that I made first when I heard this, because I felt, or I misunderstood, simple to mean easy. Simplicity is always extremely difficult to achieve. In fact, great artists, musicians, dancers, they know how difficult it is to bring simplicity into their style, into their performance. So, please don't confuse simple with easy. It is simple because it is not complicated. That means the process is very simple, like adding milk to water, it's a very simple thing, or like walking, it is very simple. Now, walking is not only simple, but it's also natural, but we all know that as human beings we had to learn to walk when we were children. That it was simple, that it was natural, did not mean it did not have to be learnt. So, meditation is something like that: it's very simple, it's also natural, but it's not very easy to do, until we know how to do it. It is necessary to emphasize this, because many people come, they hear it is very simple and then afterwards they get disappointed when they don't find it so easy. So, this confusion between simple and easy, we should not have in our minds right from the beginning.

Now, what is the problem with meditation? The problem is that it is so simple that it is easy to make mistakes. It is like walking, it is so simple that often we stumble and fall, because we don't attend to what we are doing. So, the first important thing is that meditation needs attention. Now, my Master Babuji Maharaj, Shri Ram Chandraji as he was known, used to try to pinpoint this for us when we were beginners. He often used to say that meditation is such a natural thing that we are doing it all the time, without knowing that we are doing it. He defined meditation as "thinking about something continuously." And he told me when I first met him, that if you think continuously about something, it is in fact meditation on that something about which you are thinking.

The problem is, we have all been meditating all our lives on various things without in fact knowing that we have been meditating on them. And the whole thing is complicated, because when we talk of meditation, it assumes either religious overtones or some sort of esoteric overtones which are not intended. And my Master always said "Meditation is as easy, as natural as breathing." So I asked him, "Then, why have we to learn it?" His explanation was, that a child learns its mother tongue naturally, without learning the language, but anybody else has to learn the language. But it also is a true thing that children who learn their own language are rarely scholars in that language. You have only to see the farmers, the lorry drivers, the bus people, to know that even though they are Frenchmen, they are not French scholars. So, to achieve perfection in their own language, even their own mother tongue, they have to study it. So, there is this difference that one who can speak the language because he was born into it, has the natural ability to speak just that much that is necessary to carry him through life; but to achieve perfection, study is necessary, devoted study, dedicated study, continuous study. So, like that, even though we are all meditating naturally on so many things, when we want to achieve perfection, we have to be taught to do it all over again.

That is in a general way, but now we come to the difference between one meditation and another, because meditation only means to think continuously about something. And without knowing it, we think about one thing continuously, because that is what is occupying our minds, that is what we want to achieve. And generally this endeavour of natural meditation without knowing we are meditating is restricted to our material aspirations. And we have not realised that we get that upon which we meditate, though that is what really happens. So, this fact has also to be taught to us, that we meditate on that which we want and we get that on which we meditate. This simple but unknown fact, generally unknown fact, has been put in occult language. "As you meditate, so you become." So what is the difference when we come to an institution like this and we start to meditate? The difference is only on what we want to become, and on what we are going to meditate. The law that we get that upon which we meditate, is an inviolable law and here, in such organizations like ours, where divinisation is the goal, obviously the object of meditation has to be appropriate to that goal.

Now, all this rather lengthy introduction is because many people come who have been meditating on other things, and ask, "Why should we have a new meditation which you are teaching?" Now, the method is not new, because meditation is always meditation, the difference is in what we meditate upon. That too does not seem to be very easy to understand, because many people meditate on mantras, many people meditate on forms and many people on different gods. For instance Christians on Christ, Buddhists on Buddha, things like that. But if we remember again the old or ancient law that we can only become that upon which we meditate, we can easily see the difference. So, while the process is always the same, the object is different, the goal is different. Therefore we have so many systems and we must have so many systems. We have so many languages, but in all the languages we say the same things. For instance, I can say, "I am hungry," in so many languages. The languages are different, but the thoughts they convey are always the same. Here it is different: meditation is always the same process, but depending on what we meditate upon, the goal is different, what we become is different. It is like taking a bicycle and four boys start bicycling, but all in different directions, they get to different places.

Please don't think I am oversimplifying the explanation because it is necessary. Because I find wherever we go, there is a lot of confusion about meditation. People come and say, "I am also meditating, why do you come and ask me to meditate on

Sahaj Marg method?" Now, that is what I have been trying to explain to you, that the word meditation is one, the process is the same, but because the object upon which we meditate is different, the goal is different. Therefore, we are all meditating but becoming different things, achieving different things.

It is like saying, "I am eating." Twenty people are eating, they are eating different things, some good, some bad, some poisonous, therefore the effect is different on us. Now, in Sahaj Marg, which is what our system is called, which means the natural way, the simple way, the goal is only one, and that is the perfection of the human condition approaching divinisation. Therefore, the object has to be appropriate to that goal. My Master always said, "If you meditate on power, you become powerful,"—what happens in many paths of meditation or yoga, where the object is *shakti*, which in Sanskrit is just power. Many of you may have read the Hindu or the Indian texts, and would have been familiar with rishis who meditated for—not rishis exactly, but so many people who meditated even for hundreds of years, and all they got was weapons to fight wars with, or powers extraordinary. I mean, Hindu mythology is full of such stories. Few of them ever went beyond this level to divinisation. Not because it was not available or because it was not possible, but because they did not want it.

Now, this is what happens in our modern life too. We are all meditating all the time. In fact we are meditating with so much passion and concentration of the mind that it is really extraordinary. We are able to bring our minds to one point, on one subject and we become experts on that subject. It may be science, it may be the humanities, it may be wealth, it may be love, it may be anything. But all of it is restricted to the material world. Therefore, we find this rather unnatural division that there we think about something, while here we say we are meditating, though the thing is the same! And therefore the word meditation has become restricted to some sort of religious context, which as far as Sahaj Marg is concerned is a very unfortunate confusion.

Because Sahaj Marg has nothing to do with religion at all. My Master says, "It is a universal system, which can be practised by all human beings anywhere." It uses the mind to regulate the mind, until the mind becomes a perfect instrument over which we have control. We use it for the purpose of meditation. And the object, because it is divinisation and my Master says, "God can have no name, no form, no attributes," therefore it is not the God of any particular religion—it is the Absolute, which has no name. And in fact one of the fundamental sayings of my Master is that only where religion ends, spirituality begins. And this is the science of spirituality where meditation is undertaken with the purpose of divinisation. So, the confusion that meditation is something with a religious context, that is why I said, it is unfortunate.

So, we have the possibility of saying there are three types of meditation: the meditation on material objects and material success; meditation using objects of religions, religious worship, such as the gods of religions, like you can meditate on Christ or the Buddha—which is actually something of an anachronism I should say, because you are trying to be in religion, but are really out of religion when you are meditating. To my mind, it is actually a contradiction, because the object of spirituality is to rise beyond religion, but here we are getting stuck into the religion itself.

And then, we come to the third one, where the meditation is on something which transcends religion, where therefore the object of meditation cannot be a particular god of any religion, but which conforms to the definition that the Absolute Reality has no name, no form, no attributes. So, that is how we come to the third stage of meditation, you see, the meditation on the material objects, meditations on the gods of religion, meditation on the Absolute.

In Sahaj Marg we are trying for this third objective of divinisation. That is why my Master offers it as a universal system, with this caution that it cannot or should not be used for material benefits, nor should it be restricted to any particular religion. But at the same time, please understand, this does not criticize those who have only material aims and objects in life, nor does it want to take away anybody from his or her religion; all that he says is, if you stick to material life you are going to be doomed to disappointment, because however much you may achieve, there is no satisfaction, there is no completion. So, the material pursuit is doomed to failure because at no stage can you rest and say, "Yes, I have achieved." So, there is no satisfaction in a material pursuit.

The second thing is, that material things are doomed to destruction; in the course of time, everything goes. And the most important thing is the third thing, that when you die you cannot take them with you. So, that shows the, if you don't mind my saying so, absurdity of focusing our goal on the material life.

(p.203-209)

— ❖ —

So, here we have a very practical system which has very little philosophy behind it, no esoteric teachings, no theology, things like that. So, what we do here is to sit down and meditate. Nothing else is essential to make progress. We have books for those who like to read them, but it is not essential, because a knowledge of theory can only help the practice, not substitute for the practice. The practice is the main thing. So, we come to this important fact that when we meditate we achieve something, depending on what we meditate upon. In this system the goal is called variously as human perfection or realisation or divinisation, all abstract, therefore the object must be abstract.

Therefore, Sahaj Marg does not use any names, or mantras or forms for meditation, but because the ordinary human being cannot meditate on the abstract, my Master uses Divine light as the closest to the abstract principle, because light has no form, light has no substance even, light has no—well, practically nothing to it. And my Master once explained it, or rather one of his preceptors explained it, that it is like using a diving board in a swimming pool to dive. It gives us something on which we can gain a little momentum before we take off and dive into the pool. Therefore, light is not the goal of our meditation, please remember that. It is only the starting point of the system: accepting the human limitation that we cannot directly meditate on the abstract.

So, that is a general statement of what Sahaj Marg is. And I will recapitulate by saying, we meditate to achieve divinisation, and the object is as abstract as possible, which is light in the heart... (p.210-211)

— ❖ —

Fortunately, in meditation, the practice also is simple. Meditation leading to realisation. We make it complicated by having so many objects of meditation, like material growth, material prosperity, health, success, and also God. Now people may ask, "What is wrong with this?" My Master said, "Nothing is really wrong, but if at one time you are trying to achieve fifty different objectives, your mind's power is divided into fifty different channels. Therefore, we have to try to achieve one thing at a time." (p.213)

— ❖ —

So we are trained to accept reality through meditation. Through perception, we do not accept reality, we only perceive. (p.258)

— ❖ —

Q: We should try to meditate on the Master instead of the light in the heart?

A: Only when the thing comes spontaneously.

Q: Because I don't think any more about...

A: It's not a question of what we think. You must always start with light in the heart. I told you this in Vorauf also in '85, that a time comes when, automatically, you will find the Master's figure or form. That is the right time to meditate.

Q: Yes, but I don't mean on the form. Trying to establish contact with the Master in the heart instead of only light in the heart.

A: No, no, but the light in the heart is...

Q: Is the Master.

A: Yes, but until he reveals himself as the Master... you see, it is like you and your wife. Your wife is your neighbour—I mean, you have lived together all your lives, and one day you suddenly marry her and discover she's your wife. Isn't it? Till then, she was only the neighbour's daughter.

Q: Because this, I cannot meditate on this idea of the light in the heart anymore. The feeling is that this light which I don't think of is the Master that is in my heart.

A: No, no, that is an intellectual idea. Isn't it? That the light is the Master.

Q: No, he says he doesn't meditate on the light in the heart, he just has the idea, as I understand it, he has the idea that the Master is in his heart, without an image.

Q: Without any image of his physical form.

A: But what are you meditating on then?

Q: The presence of the Master in the heart.

A: That is not correct. You must either meditate on the light in the heart, or the form of the Master, full form, not only just the face; or, when that goes, then comes the third stage when there is nothing to meditate on. There meditation stops. Otherwise you are meditating on a thought—on an idea, you see.

Q: But I feel it. I feel this presence in the heart, it's not a thought.

A: No, no, you feel the presence, that's all right. You see, like, you know, I am sitting here. I feel the presence of the cook in the kitchen. So what? Feeling the presence of... I feel the presence of money in the bank, but it's not my money. I see people are coming and depositing vast sums, others taking away money. I feel the presence of food on the streets, like today we saw someone eating and drinking. What is it to me? So the Master must become mine, you see. Established permanently, not just during meditation. And if you feel his presence in the heart, then he must be there always. Isn't it?

Q: So, either the light in the heart or the form.

A: Yes, and one leads automatically to the other. You try to meditate on the light and see what happens.

Q: Does it lead necessarily to the other?

A: Yes, one day you don't find the light, you find the Master.

Q: The form, not the essence, you mean.

A: No, no, the form is there. I mean, suppose you had never seen Babuji. What would you say, who is your master? He was still there, somewhere, but he is not your Master. So the form comes only to say, "I am your Master." If you accept him.

Q: There are days when I find it easier to meditate on the form than on the light, and days when I find it easier to meditate on the light than on the form.

A: That only means you are still vacillating between two things. It is not a question of easier, it comes. Like some day I think of money and I think of dollars; on other days I think of the stupid Indian rupee which has no worth. Money is money.

Q: So when the form comes, we meditate forever on the form.

A: Yes, absolutely forever on the form.

Q: We cannot come back to the light in the heart.

A: No. It is not necessary, you see.

Q: So you cannot meditate on the essence of the Master before this appearance of the form of the Master. It doesn't happen that way.

A: It is a projection—not real. It is like I told you, you know, if you ask a class of schoolboys, sixteen years old, "Think of your wife." What would they think of? A wife is only an idea at that time, you see. Or, each one may have some funny idea, you know, one thinks of Gina Lollobrigida or something like that. And she's not his wife. The wife is the reality, you see. For a bachelor, the reality has not yet come into his existence. He may have so many imaginations of what his wife should be like, or what he wants her to be like, but when the marriage takes place, that is the reality. (p.263-266)

— ❖ —

...we should remember that even meditation must be with love. But if you approach meditation with the idea of getting something from the Master, again it becomes a commercial transaction. Then we have this idea, "Oh, I have been meditating for six months, I have got nothing." Somebody says, "I have meditated for two years, I have got nothing." But we forget that we don't meditate to get something, we meditate to become something. (p.306)

— ❖ —

...that is the way of experiencing divinity. Not through the five senses, but by transcending the five senses. Therefore, the way of yoga meditation is to progressively nullify the senses. We sit in a particular way which we call an *asana*. We close our eyes, and turn the entire attention inwards.

Initially, of course, we are a bit confused, we are a bit bewildered. Because the whole tendency of human existence is to look outwards to see things, to perceive things, to experience things. We are always told, "Keep your eyes and ears open. Be attentive." So, this tendency is to project oneself outwards. And the more outward projected we are, the more aware we are supposed to be. So unfortunately, awareness, concentration, these also are things which you only exteriorize, focus on the outer world, and forget the inner. And we are always told, "Concentrate on this," or "concentrate on that," which is concentration on an object or a thing.

So you see, when the ordinary human being, average human being is asked to meditate by turning his attention inwards, it is a total reversal of our normal tendencies of life, and we have the additional problem that we have to look at something which doesn't exist physically. When we are told to meditate on God and we are told that God has no form, name, attributes, we are confused, naturally. That is why people find religion and religious practices, religious search for God, far easier to do, though by and large nothing more is achieved than a certain state of mind, peace of mind. (p.310)

— ❖ —

Q: Can we start meditating again while being in the group once meditation is over and that Master is there.

A: Does it mean that you can sit here again in meditation? Normally, my Master used to say that if you have time you can meditate as many times as you like every day provided you meditate one hour at a time and no more. But when you are in a group it is etiquette to follow the program. (p.313-314)

— ❖ —

Q: Sometimes, I think due to practice, I feel physically and mentally completely tired and exhausted. Why? What to do?

A: It is my general experience that people who are already tired get more tired when they sit down to meditate. Meditation cannot possibly make anybody tired. On the contrary, it has been my personal experience that on some occasions I have been working, even three days, four days with practically no sleep. Especially when I used to travel with my Master. And then the fourth day or the fifth day he would give me a sitting for ten minutes and I would be fresh as a baby. No tiredness, no exhaustion. So how can meditation make us tired? It's a wrong conception. What to do? Well, try to do less in your daily life.

(p.316)

Q: It is preferable during meditation to put the Master in your heart rather than putting yourself in the heart of Master, could you explain this to me please.

A: Both are wrong. You are not supposed to put the Master in your heart. You are supposed to meditate on the light in the heart, and if we develop to the level where one day the Master appears in the heart—appears in the heart, not you put him—then it is appropriate to meditate on his form. I have never heard of the abhyasi putting his form in the heart of the Master for meditation. In any case, it's very wrong. (p.318)

— ❖ —

The lesson is, at least start now. And don't wait until you are seventy-six. So there is no problem, you see. And this is based on something my Master once told me. He said, "Old people are generally senile and too weak to do any real yoga and meditation. But if they come to me I give them out of compassion because they are too old to get anything for themselves." (p.319)

— ❖ —

...my Master always said that the time spent in doing hatha yoga can be more profitably spent in doing meditation...

...Another thing is, by doing yoga properly, I mean, raja yoga—meditation—the body is also maintained at an optimum level of fitness. We don't need to be superlative giants. The body is maintained as is necessary to maintain it.

So if we do the meditation and the cleaning systematically, automatically the physical and the mental and the psychic fall into patterns that they have to adopt, obeying the law that the higher governs the lower. If you start with the lower, you cannot affect the higher. So even for things like personal health, it's better to do meditation correctly. There is no special or specific need to do any physical exercise, hatha yoga, things like that.
(p.321-322)

Heart to Heart, Volume III
Shri P. Rajagopalachari

Please do not expect just one meditation to prove anything to you. Because in this system of meditation we do not get anything. It helps us to lose, progressively, all that we have accumulated inside ourselves until, as I said, we become so subtle that the inner subtlety and the outer subtlety must match. And we can say, "*Voilà!* It is this." So this invitation to meditate should not be treated as a test or a trial, you know, like a sample of a product. But I hope you will feel something which may bring you closer to what you are seeking and persuade you to follow it further. Thank you. (p.25)

— ❖ —

Now very often in the West when we come here and we sit and say, "We are going to meditate. Please close your eyes. Sit comfortably," there are always some persons who come and ask, "How can you achieve anything sitting quietly with your eyes closed?" This question is inevitable and it is understandable because I had the question myself in my mind. How on earth can you do anything sitting down with your eyes closed?

In fact, my Master once told me that his mother once accused him, saying, "You are sitting with your eyes closed and fooling yourself. And not only are you fooling yourself, you are fooling the others who come to you." And then she asked him one famous question, "Have you seen that which you are trying to show to them?" So you see, his mother could not believe that it was possible. His father thought he was crazy because he had no ambition, he had no interest in money, he had no interest in books, "Just sitting under a tree closing your eyes and lost to this world" And when he came back, if you asked him, "What have you got?" he had nothing to show. What can you show which is inside yourself? (p.36)

But the point is, how did I come to this understanding that a master must love without judgment? Through my practice, because when you look inside yourself in meditation, inevitably you find all the ugly things, the dirty things, the stupid things inside. There have been occasions, during meditations, when I have had so much nausea that I have had to vomit physically. I was nauseated with myself. Now when you are exposed to your inner condition, you see, outside you can clean and, you know, polish and paint. What about **this** inside here?

You remember the story of Christ when an adulterer was about to be stoned to death by the evil laws of those days. He came and he said, "Let him cast the first stone who has not sinned." And he said something more. He said, "Sinning is not only of the body. The sin starts with the mind." He was very explicit. He said, "If you have lusted after a woman in your mind, it is a sin." So when my Master taught me to go into myself—I mean, there is nothing I am exposing, because if you go into yourself, you are going to find the same things. The same things about which we are ashamed, which make us crazy, miserable, hate ourselves and which self-hatred is the cause of most of the broken marriages of the world today. Now when you find this in yourself, how can you possibly blame anybody else? Because if there is anything, I am worse than everybody else. This is what we feel. (p.39)

— ❖ —

So today, my dear sisters and brothers, I have put together my Master's life and his teachings. The practical aspect of it is a very simple thing. We meditate. Now, what is meditation? My Master said, "When you think continuously about something, it is meditation." And he said, "All of us are meditating all the time." Somebody is meditating on money, somebody on his girlfriend, somebody on the power that he wishes to achieve. And therefore they achieve that because they are meditating on that. They are not just thinking about it. All that we do here is meditate on something higher than all these things, the Self in the form of light in the heart and, through that, progress stage by stage to the ultimate revelation of the reality within us. (p.49)

— ❖ —

I remember, I visited one of the ashrams of one of the great Indian organizations with connections in France. I met an old lady there about forty-five or fifty years old. This was twenty years back. I had come with my spiritual Master, Shri Ram Chandraji Maharaj. He was talking with the head of the ashram and I was walking in the garden, because maybe they were having a private talk, I do not know. I met this old lady and we started talking. I told her I meditate and I asked her, "How much do you meditate?" She said, "I have not started meditation yet." I asked her, "How long have you been here?" under that particular system, you see. She said, "Twenty-three years." I said, "What have you been doing these twenty-three years?" "Oh," she said, "my guru told me we need a lot of preparation before we can meditate. So I spent three years in the kitchen cutting vegetables, three years in the washing room washing clothes, three years in the infirmary with patients and, after all that, now I am doing gardening work to teach me patience." I asked, "When will you start meditation?" She said, "When my guru permits." See, this a very tragic thing; and when I told my Master about it, he was not only extremely surprised, he was anguished to see how people are being misled. (p.76-77)

— ❖ —

...my Master taught that we should, "Begin straight with meditation." So here we come back to the old Indian tradition of raja yoga, which has been there for thousands of years. The last three stages of what is called Pantanjali's *ashtanga* yoga: *dharana, dhyana,* and *samadhi*. All the rest is preparation. A preparation which may be necessary for some but not for all. If you are normal and if you desire to practise meditation, well, now is the time to begin...

...Initially, it was a big mixture of hatha yoga, raja yoga, *pranayama*, everything. But I think, subsequent to the development of the *bhakti* path there was a tendency among raja yogis, that is the practitioners of raja yoga, to progressively move away from the emphasis on the body and its parts until you come to a refined state where you just sit in a comfortable pose, which you can maintain for the period of your meditation, and start meditating...

So with the people, who were really interested in spiritual development, no longer interested in the powers of the body, or even the mind, they came to the pure form of raja yoga, meditation and nothing else. (p.78-79)

— ❖ —

In meditation, we use the mind to purify itself, refine itself, regulate itself. That is why it is, sometimes, very difficult to understand how we can possibly meditate and achieve all these things. Because it is using the mind itself to work on itself, to purify and refine itself. In the beginning it looks very confusing, but we must remember that is how everything is done. We use a weak body to make it stronger by exercise. We use a weak intellect to work upon itself, to strengthen it until it becomes a magnificent intellect. So there is really no problem in using the mind itself to refine itself, to purify itself, to regulate itself.

And in raja yoga, as taught by my Masters, which is a continuation of the famous traditions of Ramanuja and Kabir especially, you see, the emphasis shifts to the heart. And now there is no more tension, no more exercising. You just try to bring the Divine presence into the heart, or rather to realise Its presence there.

So meditation shifts from points (like the point between the eyebrows, the point of the nose, they are the traditional points of meditation), to meditation on the heart. And it is a funny thing, if you study the life of the old rishis of India, they are supposed to have meditated on these points for thousands of years, somehow.

And their meditation was so successful that they could bring the god on whom they meditated in their presence. They could ask for anything, the highest being the power of that divinity. And they got it. And tradition says they destroyed themselves with those powers. (p.81-82)

— ❖ —

...we begin with *dhyana*. The idea being to focus the mind on one object of meditation, taking care to see that the object is not something solid, something without a form, because the effect of our meditation is conditioned or, shall we say, limited by the object that we choose to meditate upon. "As you meditate, so you become," this is a well-known old occult proverb.

So, in our system, we meditate on the abstract, no names of God, no forms, no mantras. But, at the same time, because it is impossible to meditate on nothingness, my Master suggests we meditate on light in the heart, something nearest to divinity. In its own way it is formless, attributeless, nameless, because the goal of the Sahaj Marg system is ultimate union, if possible, with the Absolute, which incidentally is what yoga really means. (p.103)

— ❖ —

I asked my Master, "What is the need to do meditation then?" Because, suppose you are in love with somebody, you do not have to meditate to fall in love. And he laughed. He said, "It is a discipline which is necessary. Because human beings have so little discipline, personal discipline, I suggest meditation and all these things as a discipline to train yourself in obedience, to train yourself to bring your mind under regulation, remembering that a fully regulated mind yet cannot take you to God realisation, but is useful in other ways, for instance in research, even in yoga, and things like that." And I said, "Meditation on the heart, thinking of the divine presence there, by remembrance, it develops love." See, here comes his great technique, that we call constant remembrance. He was always saying, that, "We remember those whom we love." By reversing the technique, by remembering, we can create love for the one remembered in our hearts. So the meditation of the Sahaj Marg system is a technique to create remembrance of the Beloved, thereby creating love for the Beloved, and then He steps in and says, "Welcome." So that is why we have meditation. (p.110)

— ❖ —

I remember the first time I went deep into meditation, what you call *samadhi*. It took Babuji several minutes to recall me out of it. He said, "That's all." I did not open my eyes. He said it several times, louder and louder. And finally he had to touch me. Then I asked him what happened. He said, "That is an experience which you should have at death. What we really do in meditation is to learn to die." So I told him this would be a very difficult thing to teach to people, because who wants to die? They want training in how to live—more joyously, more healthily, more richly. He said, "They are fools, because they do not know the secret that, unless you know how to die, you cannot live." And it is such a simple truth, you see. Because one of the greatest, most prevalent modern diseases is fear of death. And it manifests itself in so many ways. So when we go deep into meditation, Babuji told me, "But for the grace of the Master, you would not have come back today." I said, "Why did you bring me back?" He just smiled and kept quiet. He said, "But it is a fact that when you went into that level your soul did not want to come back. Therefore, it took me four minutes to wake you up again. Because that is its original state, its real state, its natural state."

...So when I said that meditation teaches us to die, it teaches us by showing us that there is no real death. It is a state of existence which we call death. But the moment you get into meditation, and go deeper and deeper into that condition, and the Master's grace brings you up, again and again, out of it, we learn the truth about life and death. That is real, this is artificial. I have known abhyasis weeping when they have come out of meditation and prayed to Master, "Why do you not leave me there? Why do you bring me here and torture me again?" Babuji used to sympathize. He said, "Yes, I know your state. I can understand your mental condition, but it is not permitted to shorten your life like that. But I am happy you had this experience because it is this experience which will divert your mind away from this silly, stupid material existence." (p.123-124)

— ❖ —

And eventually, like that famous example of the cave in Plato's *Republic,* you have become so accustomed to your little presence that, when the master comes with the key to open the door, you are prepared to invite him in, and say, "Come Babuji. Enjoy our life, see how nice it is here," but you are not prepared to go out with him. Now this is what happens when you come for meditation for half an hour and then go back to the other twenty-three hours of your own activities, fooling yourselves that you can make it. (p.125-126)

— ❖ —

We have a shortage of time. We have too much of time. We waste time. We utilize time. All these terms and concepts apply essentially to a material existence. Before I came to my Master I used to study some of these ancient texts of the Indians, and it was always, to me, something unbelievable that a rishi could meditate for twenty-five thousand years or fifty thousand years, when a whole human lifetime could not be measured in more than one hundred and twenty years, or even if you want to stretch it to unimaginable limits, two hundred years, four hundred years. But it made sense to me when my Master explained certain aspects of yoga, that when we are able to sit in meditation and go into the depths or our being, we can achieve, it is difficult to say what is that achievement, we can **become**, or evolve into, something which could have taken thousands of years.

And one of the first experiences I had at his holy feet, my Master's feet, was to meditate in his presence. When I had been meditating for nearly one and a half hours and when he said "Stop," I thought it had been just five minutes. And he was very amused. He said, "Look at your watch. You have got a wrist watch?" So what had seemed to me to be five minutes was really one and a half hours. On another occasion I meditated for five minutes. It felt, to me, as if I had been meditating for years, and my Master said, "This is the subjectivity of the nature of time. So do not measure your existence by hours and days and minutes. True life is lived and measured in what it achieves." (p.156-157)

— ❖ —

So yoga, raja yoga especially, says, "Sit down." There is a very simple technique to bring your mind under your regulatory apparatus, your control. Slowly train it to apply itself to one thought, and that is meditation. Unfortunately, many people say many thing about meditation. And I think the Sanskrit literature itself has to take a substantial degree of blame for it, where instead of talking of meditation, it talks more of concentration. And we hear this cry from human being after human being, "How can I concentrate? My mind is not mine you see. I cannot think of something for two minutes and you are asking me to concentrate." Now, my Master explained this very beautifully. He said, "Meditation is to think continuously of something. It is a process. You have to make the effort and progressively, as you are able to hold your mind on that thought for longer and longer periods of time, you come to a state where the mind is totally on that, you see, and that is concentration." (p.163)

— ❖ —

Now you may not find it easy to believe, but I can tell you many of the abhyasis of my Master, his disciples, have been able to reach a state of *samadhi* within a few months of their starting their practice. Whereas, if you read the traditional yogic literature of India, you read that Vishwamitra meditated twenty-five thousand years, Vasishta meditated fifty thousand years. We are confused, you see. "How is it possible? Am I really in a state of *samadhi*?" And yet it is a fact. It happens, you see, because when you do something right, how much time should it take to give you the result? It should not take any time at all. As my Master said, "If you know how to meditate, the instant you close your eyes you should be in *samadhi.*" And perhaps you will permit me to say, that nowadays I am very often in this situation that, if I close my eyes, I am liable to slip into *samadhi* and not wake up again. This started soon after I started my Master's method.

I was in a music performance and my wife was sitting next to me listening to the music. I closed my eyes and when my wife shook me awake the concert was over. She was very angry with me. She said, "You know everybody was looking at you. You come to an expensive concert and you are sleeping here." I could never convince her that I was not sleeping. And when I told my Master about this, he laughed. He said, "The explanation is so simple. By meditation you have trained your mind to concentrate. Now when you concentrate on something the mind goes into a state of absorption, and there you are. That is what happens."

So you see, Sahaj Marg is a system which can give you this state, which is so highly praised in Patanjali's system, the culmination of yogic endeavour, the eighth and final step, *samadhi.* My Master used to think not very highly of *samadhi*. He said, "What is the use of *samadhi*? All right, you have achieved it. You have seen it. What is the use of it? If you go into *samadhi* and come out of it the same person who went into it, it is as good as a dirty man going into a river and coming out as dirty as he went in." So, in our system of Sahaj Marg as it is called, the natural way, there is very little value for the state of *samadhi,* except as an indicator that you now have your mind very much under your regulation. And as my Master used to say, "Now begins true yoga." So meditation, *samadhi*, these are states, you see, which have no real relevance to evolution. And my Master's conviction was that all the yogic research of the past had stopped at *samadhi* and not gone beyond it. That is what he has been teaching us. (p.164)

— ❖ —

Sensitivity is being conscious of what is happening **to** us, not necessarily of what is happening around us. When we first become sensitive, naturally we are sensitive only to that to which we are ordinarily exposed, which is the outer world. So we hear things more clearly and even if a spoon drops, the meditation is disturbed. But as the attention goes inwards, then sensitivity starts working in our favour. We become more sensitive to the inner reality, and then whatever the noise, this does not disturb us. So sensitivity is good, but it is troublesome if you continue to remain attracted to the outside world.

I would like to say some more things about, a few more words about, sensitivity which you will not find in books. This is my personal experience. When I started meditation, I used to be quite disturbed by a lot of things. As I was saying, even if a spoon falls on the ground, it is as if, you know, there is an explosion somewhere. And naturally, when you are disturbed you become irritated and that breaks your meditation. And I used to get up and go away. So we have no sadhana like that. I know women know this thing very well, that when the husband is sometimes very angry, even when they are eating they get up and go away. In India it is very common. They just get up and walk away. You can eat afterwards. But meditation lost means it is lost. (p.181)

— ❖ —

Once when I was talking to Babuji, there was another abhyasi with us who had volunteered for service during Basant. He came to Master and said, "Babuji, I am not able to do any sittings. I am on this and this duty, and I am here only for three days. I do not have the benefit of your blessings. What is the use of my coming for Basant?" Just on the spur of the moment, even though he was addressing my Master, I said, "That which you can earn by service you cannot get even by *sadhana*, because we do not have the ability, we do not have the moral fibre, in today's world, to be perfect *sadhaks*. It is not possible."

First of all, we bring with us such a load of samskaras that even to sit and meditate, it requires the blessing of the Master. So many people are here who have written to me, in their reports and their letters, "I do not find the time to meditate. I am unable to do the evening cleaning. I am not able to meditate, sometimes, even once a month."

So you see, it is not a play or a game that somebody decides to meditate, and he or she is able to meditate. Even for **that**, you require His blessings. It is not something that every person can do, even among our abhyasis. I think this problem faces at least eighty percent of all abhyasis, to my personal knowledge. Eighty percent of about twenty-five thousand abhyasis, you can imagine, who cannot be regular, not because they do not want to be, but they are unable to be. Either their spouse is troubling them, or their parents are, or their families, or their children, or their jobs. (p.218-219)

— ❖ —

Sahaj Marg has always said, you see, balanced existence, two wings of the bird. Again, very nice quotations. Whenever people quote these words of my Master they are quoting it in a self-convenient way of wishful thinking. Yes, He has permitted me to do this, and that too. And 'that too', of course, applies to meditation. You know we can live a nice life and continue our meditation. Yes, but we are only emphasizing the next life. The good cars, the happy holidays. What about the meditation? "Oh, but you know, I cannot meditate. My husband says, 'Do not meditate'." Why not? Do you listen to your husband in everything that you do? Why only in meditation do we have to sacrifice our personal interests? Do not women have love affairs? Do they ask their husband's permission to go out with somebody else? Or do men ask their wive's permission to go and sleep with somebody else? Why only for meditation, the wife should interfere? (p.225)

— ❖ —

So we come to this second aspect of the tradition, of the yogic tradition, that there was once a time when people meditated on the point of the nose, the *nasikagre* as they called it, *bhruvor madye*, the point between the eyebrows, perhaps on the point of the navel, when you take the *shat* chakras, the six chakras around the spine. But tradition itself says they got some *vara prasada*, as we call it, some gift from the god to whom they worshipped, which was generally power-oriented, a weapon, an invincible weapon, the ultimate weapon, perhaps. And as my Master once said, "There are weapons in the yogic arsenals before which the atom bomb and the neutron bomb are as nothing." We have the tradition in India that great people meditated for these weapons and ultimately they destroyed themselves with those weapons. Because against divinity, a weapon which divinity itself gives you, or confers upon you, in return for your *tapasya*, as meditation is called, cannot be used. (p.262)

— ❖ —

I remember once I asked my Master, Babuji Maharaj, "What is the real use of this, *asanas* and *pranayama?*" He said, "I will tell you something which perhaps you have never heard before. Will you believe it?" I said, "Certainly, you know I cannot possibly disbelieve." I did have reservations in my mind. He said, "This system of yoga was created by ancient rishis who had to meditate twenty-four hours a day in their caves up in the Himalayas. They could not go for a walk. They could not go for a swim. They could not practise calisthenics. Therefore, they evolved a system of yogic practice, in which seated as they are in meditation, they changed their postures periodically and kept the system revitalized periodically."

And the breathing, *pranayama*? Well, anybody who has meditated knows this is the matter of practical experience, that when you meditate, and you go into deep meditation, the breathing practically stops. So the system needs oxygen, you see. It is a vital necessity. It is called the *prana vayu* in Sanskrit, the life-giving gas. So they develop this *pranayama* to slowly breathe in and out, keep the system replenished with the oxygen. All with only one purpose in mind, that I have to be alive until I reach my destination. No more, you see. (p.272-273)

— ❖ —

There are levels of rishis. To call everybody a rishi is a stupid thing. So the highest level of rishi is the *Brahma* rishi. One who has made the *Brahma,* the ultimate principle, his own, he worships Him in the heart. And he and He, there is no difference, except the notional difference yet there because this man is still alive in the human form. And there is this, what we say in Hindi, the *parda*, you see, the veil of this-ness and that-ness which still separates us. And how did they do it? Meditation! How did Valmiki who wrote the *Ramayana,* who dictated it to no less a person than Vigneshwara? Again by meditation.

Did the mantra matter? This is a very important point to notice, you see, because *tantric* traditions speaks of the need to have the sacred mantra. When he was told to pronounce the word Rama, the sacred name of Lord Rama, he could not do it. His initiator, the man who initiated him said, "It does not matter. Say mara, mara, mara." And mara, mara, mara, becomes Rama, Rama, Rama, eventually. And it is said, his meditation was so deep that the termites built a hill around him. It is called *valmika* in Sanskrit. Therefore he was Valmiki, he who was reborn out of an ant hill and he was a sage. All by meditation! (p.275-276)

— ❖ —

So it is not enough to be a human, it is necessary to be conscious. And how is that consciousness going to come unless we meditate and realise that it is so. Therefore you see meditation is the only and sole method of self-realisation. All the rest: powers, *siddhis*, yes, transcendental powers can be yours. But as the yogic masters have said again and again, Ramakrishna has said, Satya Sai Baba of today says the same thing, "Forget miracles. They are not for you. I do it as something to tempt you by, you see, to the divine part. But if you fall for these miracles, you are bound." (p.284)

In His Footsteps, Volume I
Shri P. Rajagopalachari

Mr. B said that he had some strain previously between the eyebrows and at the forehead during meditation. Today he had experienced more peace and relaxation.

Dr. K.C. Varadachari: Yes, but meditation should relieve strain. The mistake is in trying to concentrate. Real concentration comes after long practice of meditation. If you try to concentrate, you get strain. The strain may be at the eyebrows, forehead, or even at the heart. The proper way to meditate is to bring the attention on the heart at the beginning of meditation—and then proceed. Don't try to concentrate. This is the best way. If you feel any strain or tension, just relax and try to **receive** the transmission from the Master. Don't make an effort. Just relax and receive. (p.9)

— ❖ —

Dr. K.C. Varadachari: Now, why do you sit for meditation? You want peace, or happiness or whatever it is. You can't get it unless you sit in meditation. So you must sit. Now, when you sit you hear all the sounds more clearly, small things become prominent—you have to sit long enough until you hear the real sound—the soundless sound—the Voice of God!

Now think what happens when you want to listen to a favourite programme on the radio. You wait for the correct time—and also spend time tuning in correctly—and if there is static or other disturbance, you still listen to your programme with concentration, forgetting all other disturbances by a conscious exclusion of other extraneous disturbances. That is what happens here also. You must try and sit in the same place, at the same time every day, as far as possible. This helps to prepare the mind for reception of transmission. Regularity is of very great help as this mental attunement, or preparation, helps meditation to be fruitful. Otherwise, much time is spent in the preliminary stages of thought exclusion, and receptivity or sensitivity takes a long time to develop.

If a regular place and time is not possible because you travel a great deal, then you must sit at some time of the day suitable to you—but you **must** sit for half an hour at least! If no time during the day is at all suitable, then sit in meditation just before going to bed. That is the best. But don't let it become mechanical.

(p.19-20)

— ❖ —

Shri Ishwar Sahai: ...So in Sahaj Marg, we take up only the last three steps of the ashtanga yoga of Patanjali.

There too, we begin with *dhyana*—meditation, and from there go to *dharana*—concentration, and proceed to *samadhi*—absorption. We do not start with *dharana* or concentration as Patanjali does. We believe that meditation leads to concentration.

Now it is like this. We meditate on the heart; we get the idea of the heart and think about it, that is *dhyana*. If the idea goes away, we bring our attention back to the heart. So that after some time, say three months or more, of practise, a certain continuity of thought begins to be established. The mind does not wander so much. The thought of the heart remains for longer and longer periods—and then is *dharana*. At this stage begins the absorption of the mind in this one thought. We may not be aware of the single thought or even of its continuity—that is, conscious awareness may not be there—but it is there all the same. When that happens, we have arrived at the stage of *samadhi*. It is very easy and that is why it is called the easy path—the Sahaj Marg.

(p.26)

— ❖ —

Dr. K.C. Varadachari: ...In our system all that we are required to do is to sit and allow the force of the Master to work on us. That is all that is needed—to allow ourselves to be worked upon; meditation must result in peace, in *shanti*. And all that you will see in meditation is the sky. Nothing else. Any materializing of the Ultimate is the reverse of what we are aiming at. On the contrary we go beyond all forms, all names to the Ultimate. Thus tensions are removed, relaxation and a consequent peace result. That is what meditation gives. (p.152-153)

— ❖ —

Shri S.K. Rajagopalan: ...You are not asked to **imagine** God in any particular way, or form. Our system is based on meditation on the formless, attributeless Divine.

Now by meditation is meant knowing everything about something. Normally we **see** an object, or an idea from one angle, or point of view only. In meditation we try to see it from all sides and all points of view, and so to know it as completely as possible. That is the purpose and aim of meditation.

Now when the purpose, or object of meditation is God then a basic assumption as to the existence of God becomes essential. Naturally no one tries to know everything about something, the very existence of which he doubts. So in this meditation, a basic assumption that God exists is very essential. Without that we cannot proceed. (p.183-184)

He repeatedly stressed the need to 'observe the heart' during meditation.

"It is by the heart that the man lives. If the heart lives, he lives; if it stops, he stops. Therefore, the heart is the most important organ in the body, the system. That is why my Master introduces the higher consciousness into the heart; so that it may pervade the system from top to toe. That is why in this system, Master says the whole body is the heart region. It is therefore the heart that is the object of concentration, of meditation. It is the heart you must watch and observe. Please try to observe how the power of the Master works in your heart, where it flows, what it does. That is all we are expected to do. The power of the Master must be permitted to work." [Dr. K.C. Varadachari] (p.213)

— ❖ —

PR: Please explain what meditation really is.

Master: Meditation really means that the mind may be accustomed to the Centre itself, instead of working elsewhere. (p.289)

— ❖ —

Master, talking of puja said, "In puja the head must bend in submission. If you are conscious that you are doing puja, then it is not puja. When we do puja we go to beg from God. And of course He being God has everything. But if we take such a small bag with us, how much can He fill in it? Therefore it is necessary to become a proper vessel. We should become deserving." (p.304)

Religion and Spirituality

Shri P. Rajagopalachari

I believe it is at the present moment very mechanical. We come and we meditate. Many of us don't know why we meditate at all. We are worried about ethics and morality. We are worried about discipline. We are angry with them. (p.9)

— ❖ —

This problem we face with our abhyasis. "Why should I meditate?" I don't know if this question is so common in Europe, but in India we are frequently asked this question, "If Babuji is a special personality, God incarnate, why can't He liberate me without my going through these stupid processes of meditation, and cleaning, and all this nonsense?" I also used to wonder why not? It would be nice. If I could just go to Babuji once and he would say, "Well, it is finished. You are liberated." But then there is no fun in life, you see. You go for the job the first morning and you are made the Managing Director. There is no fun anymore. People don't recognize that something achieved without effort has no satisfaction for us. (p.25-26)

— ❖ —

So, when people come to Sahaj Marg, they expect experiences, "Yes, but I have been meditating for three months and I have no experience." Now, we have to train people out of this idea: that this is an experiential system. This is an evolutionary system. It is also a revolutionary system; but it is not per se experiential. Our experiences have nothing to do with our progress. If they have any value, it is in showing you what grossness you've had embedded in you, which is being released by the cleaning or the meditation process. To use a very crude example: when you vomit, you can see what you have eaten before you vomited. Nothing more. It stinks, because it has passed through your system. So the human system really makes everything stink. (p.27)

— ❖ —

So this idea of seeing something, feeling something, is bringing the human perceptions to play on a state of existence which is beyond the human level of existence. It is like trying to measure air with a metre stick. So you see we are trying to transpose one dimension of experience into another dimension of being, and suffering the consequences and saying, "I feel nothing, I know nothing, I see nothing, Sahaj Marg is a failure." Whereas the opposite is true: that so long as I can feel something, see something, I am at the lowest level of the spiritual ladder. So abhyasis should be trained to recognize this. And to know that when they continue to know, they are really only at the level of knowing. They have to go to the level of feeling. When they transcend that, they are going to a level where nothing more exists, either to be known, or to be felt. That is the real state of progress.

"Then what is this for? Why should I meditate any more?" Because you have to retain this state. It is like being born and continuing to eat all your life so that you will continue to live. So, at that level of growth, why you continue to meditate is for several reasons. One, because your Master asks you to do it. Second, because you need to keep the fire burning, the state retained without fall. (p.29-30)

— ❖ —

Anybody who looks at the moon sees the same moon. So, you see, from a disintegrated, diversified, lost multiplicity of characters, we try to bring them back together by meditating on the inner self, which is essentially a unity. It cannot be anything else. Why meditate? This is one of the reasons. In my external life I am many things. I am many persons. In my inner life I am one. By meditating on Him I learn, I train myself, to slowly become one personality again. (p.51)

— ❖ —

I started meditating when I was probably sixteen or seventeen years old, all by myself, from books. Because I had a natural, I don't know, I can't call it craving, it's too big a word, shall we say an affection. (p.53)

Most of us are moving like this, thinking like this, thinking round and round a problem, so that from whichever aspect you look at it, you see the same thing. Like we see the same face of the moon all the time. It's turning round us, we are turning around ourselves. ... Therefore we see the same thing all the time. We think we are thinking. But it produces no results. We are cogitating; no result. We are meditating; no result—because you are going round and round. Now this round and round—you know, we are not *tournesols* that you keep moving with the sun. We have to go straight. Round and round is useless. Straight will produce something, if at least to tell you you are going away from the goal and not towards the goal. (p.54)

— ❖ —

Spirituality teaches us to feel ourselves in our Self, by turning our attention inwards, imagining the Divine presence in the heart as brilliant light, Divine light. Slowly, by meditation, repeated meditation, deeper and deeper meditation, we can become merged in that presence. Eventually, not being conscious that you are here at all, we achieve what we call the *samadhi* state. And then you wonder what this is all about, you see. It is better to sit and meditate and be lost to this world. "It is so nice. Why did you stop the meditation?" People ask, "Why did you end the sitting? It was so wonderful. I was so absorbed. I didn't know whether I was sleeping or in the *samadhi* state." (p.71)

— ❖ —

So you see, Babuji Maharaj said, "Religions divide." When we sit in meditation, there is no God with a name, there is no God with any form. There is God without attributes. It is the absolute abstract. This unites. (p.72)

— ❖ —

Now what is there to believe in in spirituality? Religion requires belief. Religion requires faith. Spirituality requires nothing. Spirituality requires you, and your aspiration to become a perfect you. If there is an individual who is aspiring to become perfect, he is fit for spirituality. What does he need? To sit and meditate. On what? On the abstract in the heart. But how can we meditate on the abstract? Use the Divine light. Because light, according to my Master, is not, in a sense, physical. It has no form, no name, no attributes, etc., etc., it is nearest to the spiritual ultimacy. And if you are able to do that sincerely, knowing that you are going to benefit from it and nobody else, knowing that you are going to grow spiritually and nobody else—if you meditate, I cannot become spiritual. If I meditate, you cannot become spiritual.

This system of spirituality puts the responsibility back right where it belongs. Instead of becoming beggarly seekers of benefits in places of worship, praying on our knees, groveling before priests, weeping and beating our breasts with guilt, spirituality says, "My son, sit where you are. Put yourself into your heart. Meditate there. Find Him who is always there. And since He is you, how can He be anything other than what you are? How can you be anything other than what He is?" That is the moment when this flash of illumination comes, and you say, "I am everything. I am not God, but I am divine. I am God-like. I am blessed, for today, in me, I find Him whom I have been seeking throughout the universe all my life." Or so many lives, who knows, you see? (p.73-74)

— ❖ —

All our civilization, our education, our high-tech societies are only superficial. Now we have to convert this superficiality of modern technology, knowledge, wisdom, and try to embed it in our core, in the core of my being, which again is why we meditate. We meditate with a developed mind, with a conscious mind, a mind which is far more conscious today than it was say three to five thousand years ago, ten thousand years ago. And with that enlarged consciousness, with our advanced ideas of what a God must be—not just a doler-out of goodies, not just one who will say, "I pardon you," not somebody who will just eradicate all problems from my life or remove all obstructions from my path, but a God who will represent to me the ultimate goodness of existence, and pull me up to Himself—we must meditate. (p.87)

— ❖ —

As Babuji Maharaj said, "Every meditation is a training in dying." Because when you go really deep into yourself, and you come out after it, and say, "I was absorbed. I don't know where I was. I didn't even know whether I was sleeping or meditating," you have literally been not there. In a sense you were dead to this existence. Therefore, meditation is a training in dying. And if we have done it correctly, we should be masters of death, masters of the act of dying, one who can die when he wishes, one who can die when he chooses; coming back again and again if he wishes, so that his death is not really a death, but will be a resurrection like in the Christian tradition. Christ died, was put into the sepulchre, and he disappeared you see. We call it the resurrection.

So you see, if we continue to be afraid of death, it means we have not been meditating properly. Our practice has been wrong. So we should think of this, and say, "What in heaven am I doing? Have I been meditating at all? If so, have I been meditating correctly? Why am I still afraid of death?" Is not meditation a training in dying, daily? Should not one who does something daily become a master of that? Should I not by now be a master of death? Therefore, we say, "One who is a master of life is also a master of death. ...

And I repeat, if we are meditating properly, there is an absolute mastery of death that waits for us. (p.95-96)

— ❖ —

To continue with this idea of death. If it is understood in the spiritual context, it is the most remarkable, the most beautiful act of nature. Whereas we have, because of our identification with the body and its life, totally negated that original spiritual value of death, the idea of death, and converted it into something we're afraid of all of our lives. Those who have been deeply absorbed in meditation would have seen that there is nothing to be really afraid of. We are deeply merged in the inner Self. Sometimes when we wake up we don't know where we are, where we have been, how much time has elapsed. It is possible to be in that condition, even after meditation if you have the ability to hold on to that condition. Now when we come out of it, it is so blissful. We find that we have been in a state of bliss, in a state of utter peace. In fact in a state where really nothing exists, and we cannot say what has been, or what was, except to say that it was wonderful, and we are sorry it ended. (p.101)

— ❖ —

So, you see, in that sense death erases all the lost opportunities of the past. Missed opportunities, wasted opportunities, wrongly used opportunities, and puts us back once again on the field and says, "Start all over again. You are again at the beginning of the race. It can be won." So you see what a wonderful thing death really is, if we die rightly. As those who have achieved a spiritual goal in this life, we don't really die, we just sink into the deepest meditation and close our eyes. To others we are dead, but we have escaped into another dimension where we don't even know we had a body. Which is what happens in a *samadhi* condition. You fall forward, hit your head on the ground and still you don't know it. But not being used to that posture, your muscles start paining and then that wakes you up and you come up and sit erect again. And then you start falling all over again. (p.112-113)

— ❖ —

Because anybody dying with this thought of the Ultimate, with the thought of his goal in mind, reaches that goal. Anybody! To ensure that we have the right thought at the moment of oblivion, is all this problem that we are facing—meditation, constant remembrance, developing love for the Master. So that if we have established it as a continuing truth in our existence, it cannot depart from us at the moment of death. We shall die with this thought, with this condition. (p.125)

— ❖ —

Now to come back to this question of people who cannot meditate. Some are able to meditate. It doesn't mean that everybody who meditates is going to get to the goal, because it depends on what we put into it, how well we meditate, with what seriousness of purpose. Is it just a hobby? Is it just a pastime? Or is it a lifetime endeavour? Has it become my life? Am I meditating even when I am doing other things? Constant remembrance, in one sense, means that too. ...

Now what about those who cannot meditate, who have no mind to use? Are they doomed for eternity? You see, samskara has to be worked off in one way or the other. Either we have the *bhog* where we undergo the effects of the samskaras, which may be reflected as pleasure and pain, enjoyment and non-enjoyment—all the two opposites. (p.127)

— ❖ —

We meditate and make meditation a state of life, so that we are eternally in a contemplative mood, even when we are involving ourselves in other activities, which will mean minimum involvement in activities, maximum involvement in contemplation. (p.130)

— ❖ —

Satsangh with a great person liberates you. So in that sense, satsangh means to be always with. Sat—sangh. *Sat* means the truth, the eternal verity. *Sangha* means to be with. So in our meditation we are eternally with Him, or we should be if we are meditating in the right way. I am meditating upon the Divine light in the heart. The Divine presence is there, which is shedding its non-luminous luminosity. Who am **I with** when I meditate? And if I am with Him, where is my liberation? If I have been with Him through life, can I be separated from Him at death? If at death He is with me, does it not mean liberation? Can I go to hell with my God with me? ...

Have faith in what you are doing. Remember that when you meditate you are with God. Remember that when you are not meditating also He is there, because He is here (indicates the heart). My meditation is only to establish a contact with Him, like telephoning a friend and making sure he is there. Or calling, "Mummy, mummy," and she says, "Yes, darling. I am in the kitchen." This is all that is necessary. (p.134-135)

Love and Death
Shri P. Rajagopalachari

So you see teaching begins with positive instruction. "This you shall do, meditate at such and such a time." "Yes, but Chari, you know it's difficult to get up." Lost opportunity! "Yeah, but I can meditate tomorrow." It is in the future. I may not be alive tomorrow. And how do you know you'll be awake tomorrow at that time? One who cannot be awake today at that time has less possibility of being awake tomorrow at that time and even less, day after tomorrow. So as we delay, possibilities decrease. They just don't cease to exist, they go on decreasing, until a day comes when it is impossible. Impossible means possibility nil! A man who does not wake up for meditation today has less chance of waking up tomorrow at the same time, has even less the day after tomorrow. After a week he will say, "*Thik hai!* (Okay!) I managed for a week without meditation. What's so wonderful about meditation? Nothing has happened to me, I'm still the same old guy. Look at me, nothing wrong! he has been meditating, you know, like crazy. What has he got that I haven't got?"

So you see we become hardened to making possibilities impossible. (p.24)

— ❖ —

So what is worth doing must be done now, what is not worth doing should never be done.

It is not that we do what is good now and postpone the bad for the later, you see, let us meditate now and go to the pub at eleven o'clock instead of going to the pub in the morning and meditating in the evening. So you see, utilization of time means utilization of the present. (p.26)

— ❖ —

I started studying a bit of Buddhism. I was tempted to be a Buddhist because again I found the profound truth that God is within. He too meditated, he too found his final goal, his final emancipation, his *mahaparinirvana* as they say in the Buddhist religion, under the bodhi tree after forty days of meditation.

Jesus the Christ found his goal by meditation. If tradition is to be accepted, Mohammed the Prophet found his goal also by meditation. (p.68)

— ❖ —

So spirituality seeks to bring people together in an enormous transcendental synthesis of oneness of humanity, where human values have to be crystallized by practise of meditation on the heart. What are the human values? I have been talking about them so long—love, compassion, most of all. (p.72)

— ❖ —

Work enough to earn your living, enough to lead a comfortable life, enough to be moderately healthy, we don't have to be superlative he-men. Then what do we do?—I have so much more time. Meditate, because now the inner life is there. It has to begin. You did not do it when it was possible in your youth. You did not do it when it was possible as an adult. Will you be able do to it as an old man? You see, we all do our horse-riding and our walking and all these funny things when we are young because we don't know whether we will be able to do it when we are old. "Oh, but you know, when I get old Chari, I won't be able to ride a horse. Let me ride it now." But what about this inner thing? Will I be able to do it when I'm old? Will I be able to sit and meditate? Will I be able to close my eyes, or will I be lying in some hospital bed, waiting for somebody to polish me off, or in an old-age home, miserable, nobody to look after me, thinking only of my misery, meditating only on my misery, therefore becoming more and more miserable? What will I be doing?

(p.84-85)

— ❖ —

So people should know **why** they should meditate. "No, no, it gives you peace of mind." Nonsense! One Valium will put me to sleep and help me to wake up tomorrow morning better than today. Of course, if I get addicted to it, it will not help—for some people, a glass of wine, hashish. They will say, "Why meditate?" Because meditation is the only way to which you cannot get hooked in the sense that you have to take bigger and bigger doses of it. Secondly, it is something which is not external to yourself, because if it is external to yourself, today you may have it, tomorrow may not have it. (p.86)

— ❖ —

...unless your personal life can be happy, contented, stable, you have no chance of making your future a bright future oriented towards a particular goal, which we call, "the evolutionary goal." If you and your wife are always quarreling, if you and your children are always quarreling, if there is strife in the house, how can you, for heaven's sake, ever sit and meditate? Who is to think of meditation? You say, "Meditation! Come on Chari! You must be joking. Let me put my family in order." Yes, but how will you put your family in order unless you meditate and you know the value of what is in your heart and you know that by giving it, the thing grows and grows and grows. It is the only thing which grows by giving it away—the more of it you give, the more of it you have. How are you going to realise this? (p.89)

— ❖ —

Today, we don't understand ourselves, how can you understand anybody else? He who understands himself, understands everybody. One who has not understood himself or herself, can understand nothing.

How to get this understanding? Examine your heart. How to examine your heart? Sit and meditate. What do you do in meditation? Focus your attention on the heart, and then see for yourself the enormously beautiful, wonderful mysteries that are there. And once you look at that, this world becomes meaningless. It is not that we have to run away, you know, and become ascetics and celibates, but it loses its charm. Now we continue to live because we have to live, like a tree lives. I don't think a tree finds any charm in its existence, it is there because it is there—reason enough. (p.91)

— ❖ —

It is nice to sit and meditate. We feel beautiful things in meditation. We feel blissful. We lose consciousness of ourselves. We see the foretaste of that which we have to become. It is like when I go into my dining room, I take an olive and put it in my mouth—I am happy. So do you like olives? No, but I am tasting the lunch that is going to come after that. I am not tasting a single olive. I am tasting the whole lunch in that single olive. It is a promise of everything else that is to come. Similarly, the states that we experience in our meditation are the light before dawn. The sun is to rise. "Look!" "Yes, but I don't see the sun." "You will." "How do you know?" Look at that colour on the horizon. (p.123)

Revealing the Personality

Shri P. Rajagopalachari

Now I want all of you to think, to meditate: what is this that you have been breaking, and having broken, in yourself? When you find the answer, you will automatically give first priority to spirituality. Spirituality will become your life. Not another activity like shopping or going to the theatre. And this place will not be just for assembly. It will be a place of worship, where you worship with your heart He who is inside it. That is true meditation—with love, adoring Him, opening your hearts, looking inside, finding Him, making your life resplendent, beautiful, glorious, full of love. Now, we have a cup here, empty, and wine there, no cup. How are you going to drink it? So you see, this cup, which is my heart, must be emptied and then filled with the nectar of life, which is love. (p.20)

— ❖ —

Shakespeare says, "Nothing is good or bad, but thinking makes it so." So when we don't think, there are no more qualities. In meditation, we don't think. We meditate. Therefore, for one who continues to meditate and becomes, what shall we say, a sage, qualities cease to exist. (p.41)

— ❖ —

Cleaning gets rid of the past, meditation creates the future, remembrance now prevents me from indulging myself in my fancies. In His remembrance, what I do is always right. So you see, the three instruments of Sahaj Marg—cleaning, meditation, constant remembrance—in my mind, they are infallible, unbeatable, totally effective instruments. (p.54)

— ❖ —

Q: Does it mean in meditation I can find out the next step, the next step, etc.

PR: In meditation there are no steps. If you are doing it right [gestures cutting right through]—TGV. ... The steps are what we create to make it possible to understand. (p.81)

— ❖ —

Only when we allow the physical to work without our attending to it can intuition manifest. So, in meditation we do this. We are not idle. Nor are we fantasizing, but we allow our minds to be absorbed in something. The physical system is going on in its own way, in its sphere. And then the third thing comes: Divinity. So you see the beauty of meditation. Therefore, the rishis of the past have been able to talk of so many things ten thousand years ago in India, which today your scientists are discovering! But the rishi gets no credit for it, because he did not discover. He only saw it in his meditation. How can it be true? This is Occidental stupidity, Occidental bias towards themselves, Occidental racism. (p.152)

— ❖ —

Here comes the second important point—that the aim must be pure before such research will succeed. The least selfishness, or immorality of purpose, and spirituality will fail. Let us say, spirituality will not work for them. So the purpose must be moral. The physical must not interfere at any stage. Then what is the problem of meditation and revelation? Because when, through intuition, something comes to me, and when I don't even know what is coming to me, I can claim no credit for it. It is always a revelation. (p.153)

— ❖ —

We must go from plurality, to singularity, to essence. From multiplicity, to unity, to essence. From the many, to the one, to essence. From the universe, to the world, to the centre. So, always come from there, in. It is really a contraction of the self from its universal consciousness, and slowly pulling itself into the ultimate centre, which is in your heart. Initially it manifests by going out. Now it has to come in. All our lives, we have been living with an outward orientation—eyes looking outward, ears listening outwards, heart going outward, throbbing outward, you know, grasping outward. Let us now try to reverse this flow. It is what we try to do in meditation. Training the mind to come back into itself, teaching the vision, which is what really sees through the eyes—the eyes don't see. ...

So, in meditation we go towards the centre, look into the heart. To make this possible, we say, "Imagine a divine light," the presence of light there. It is a mere supposition. Why did Babuji say it is only a supposition, it's an imagination? Because it is something on which to focus my attention, and train my mind to look in. And when I have trained my mind to look in, it can plunge into the eternity without seeking an object. Because there is no object. The centre is not a place. It is not a thing. It is not a location in space or time. So, how to search for it? How to look for it? How to seek it? When? How? Why? All this is simple when we sit in meditation.

Now, what opposes this simple process? Ideally, there should be only meditation and nothing else. (p.187-188)

— ❖ —

Then he will say, "Good. Now try to make things happen." And he says, "Sit down and meditate." Babuji has emphasized that it is a passive thing. People often ask, "What do we do in meditation?" Well, we meditate. "But what do we **do** in meditation?" We meditate! "Yes, but for heaven's sake, what the hell do we **do** in meditation?" I would say, perhaps we are creating a heaven, a paradise. Try it! And then he says, "How?" Sit down. Empty your mind, clean it of all its contents—good, bad, desirable, undesirable—everything. Open the door. Be patient. "Yes, but what do I wait for?" You will know when He comes. "How should I do this?" We will help you. "What about all this blah, blah you are telling about, what did you call that 'some scary monster?'" Yes, they are very much within you—samskaras. Don't worry about them. You stop creating them. I will remove what is inside you, and make you fit as a vehicle for that which is to be put into you, to emerge and occupy its rightful position—your heart.

So you see, we are really making things happen without doing anything. I don't call God into myself. He is already there. I don't even have to clean myself. The preceptors and the Master will do it. Only, I have to submit. I have to be patient. I have to be receptive. As Babuji said, "Living death." Like a man who is facing surgery is made to look as if he is dead by being anesthetized, and then the surgeon can operate. Here, we are not anesthetized, but we are made to go into a condition where we feel the ultimate bliss of existence. And all the time the working is going on. Or to put it in better language, things are happening. What was inside is floating out. What was full is becoming a vacuum, and what was but a seed—very strangely, very surprisingly, still alive within me, over the millions of years that I have been stupid, disgraceful, truant—it starts to flower again.

(p.205-206)

— ❖ —

So you see, the only way of making things happen without doing anything, is by meditation. There is no other way. And then what happens is what He inside me—which is really 'I' inside me—which is the real me, desires. (p.207)

— ❖ —

So meditation, when we sit and we meditate, what is it that really happens? Yesterday I said, we sit, we clean ourselves, we prepare the heart to receive or welcome its transcendental occupant, its real owner, the divine essence in us which we call the soul, the *atman*, with the *paramatman* inside it, I suppose. So what we are really doing is creating a proper environment and waiting patiently for something to happen. So the crux of the matter seems to be perfecting an environment in which He can appear, and waiting for His appearance, because He is not at the beck and call of every one of us. Nevertheless, when we are able to perfect this process of purification, preparation of the environment to receive that august personality, it seems that He cannot escape coming. He has no choice, as I said yesterday. (p.218)

— ❖ —

Look inside—meditation. Don't be afraid of what you see there, because it is your own creation. Otherwise, you are like the man, you know, who created this picture, *Jurassic Park*, and goes to the movie, and runs out, frightened. He cannot see his own movie! It can happen sometimes, you see. (p.241-242)

— ❖ —

I am often asked, "What can one man meditating do to change this world? Assuming, Chari, that you are right, you know, that you close your eyes and sit and meditate. You are passive, and you are waiting for things to happen without doing anything. How can it change the world?" Why not? I have heard of avalanches in these mountains of Switzerland, where a single stone thrown somewhere set off an avalanche. Sometimes a single handclap set off an avalanche. Why not my meditation change this universe? Tell me. The strongest bridge in this world will not sustain four hundred people marching on it in step. Therefore, people who have been in the army know that when they go on a bridge, they break step. Now, they walk randomly, not left-right, left-right. If they walk left-right, left-right, they are in the water, as they say, in the drink. This is the power of vibration. The walls of Jericho, crumbling. A musician singing, and the bulbs shattering. These are all known phenomenon, accredited phenomenon, accepted phenomenon. And the latest—what they call the 'butterfly effect'—the scientists, you know. A butterfly flies off in California, violently fluttering its wings, and there is a snowstorm in Siberia.

So, don't denigrate your capacities. (p.242-243)

— ❖ —

Now, you cannot master one sense after the other. "No, no. I have mastered the sense of touch. Nothing soft will attract me any more." Something hard will attract you next.

So you see, these are not battles won by giving up one by one. The whole structure has to be demolished at the root. So, we sit comfortably, close our eyes, meditate until we are so deep, there is no more feeling, there is no sensory feeling, there is no auditory feeling, there is no tactile feeling, there is no visual feeling, and we are merged with that immensity of bliss which is inside, which is my own Self.

So, in a sense it amounts to our ability and willingness to surrender the senses. But people want meditation music. It is a modern craze. "No, no. I am used to meditating with music on." How can you do it? "I like to sit meditating with a nice girl dancing in front of me." Wonderful! And a third fellow or couple says, "We like to meditate when we are making love." You see how ridiculous it is, all this nonsense. Please, always examine these things. (p.245-246)

— ❖ —

Cyclical, going round and round until something gives you a push in a tangential direction, and you go into another sphere. That is the function of the spiritual life, and since it cannot be done from inside, it has to be done from outside. Therefore the Master! Therefore spirituality. Therefore meditation, cleaning, constant remembrance, nine o'clock prayer, etc. (p.261)

Heart of the Lion
Shri P. Rajagopalachari

Why do we meditate with our eyes closed? Many people have asked "Why can't I sit with eyes open and meditate?" Yes. Something in a miniskirt walks by and the meditation is gone! Or somebody brings a truckload of buns and wafers and ice cream—the other man's meditation is destroyed. Another one carries T-shirts and *salwar kamij*, and a third one's meditation is destroyed. So the eye is the most potent, shall we say, apparatus that we have for our guidance, and yet at the same time is potent with the possibility of degrading us, denigrating us, contributing to our fall. 'Close your eyes' is the first law of meditation. When the eyes are closed it becomes very easy to meditate.

So you see, really we don't need light for meditation. Often I am asked when I am to conduct satsangh, "Sir, should we leave the lights on in the hall?" I said, "Well, suit yourself. To me it matters not a whit. But can you sit in the light and meditate?" "No, no, we prefer dark." "Okay." You see, you actually come to state that you prefer the darkness to meditate in. Because the whole objective is to find that small sliver of light, a ray, perhaps, of light—like the ocean-going steamer looking for the lighthouse, the beam from the lighthouse to guide it to its port. In that darkness, in that immensity of our universal darkness, an internal universal darkness with which we are entombed in ourselves, all that I need is one ray of light from Him saying, "That is your destination." (p.32)

— ❖ —

So you see, we can improve upon anything by mentation, and the perfect mentation is meditation. Meditation means to think constantly about one thing. It is continuous perpetual mentation on one object. Now obviously, most of the things in this universe, or most of the items of knowledge, do not need continuous mentation, therefore need not be meditated upon.

What is it, therefore, that we have to meditate upon? That which cannot be known through the sensory apparatus that we have been furnished with—precisely. So should I meditate upon my girlfriend? No, because there are other ways of knowing her—the experiential mode. You want to know what a kiss is like? Kiss and see. (p.75-76)

— ❖ —

You don't have to speak the language of other human beings to transmit to them pain. What is pain? You pinch a little, and they know. Isn't it?

So inquisitiveness, the need to intellectually probe must be restricted to the future. And again I submit that the best way is meditation. Why? Because only through meditation I can probe into a future which is not yet physical, which is not yet sensory-conditioned, but which can be, if I am able to locate it and bring it into my present. Otherwise we are only dealing with what is already here, about which everything is known, mostly. (p.78)

— ❖ —

Don't tell the Master, "Tomorrow I will start meditation, when I go back to, I don't know, Lionsville, I will start cleaning." "When is that going to be?" "Well, I am here for three weeks in the heart clinic. Then, by your grace, if I am all right, I will go back to Lionsville, or Leopardsville or Pantherville. There I have been asked to rest for two weeks, for bed rest, by the Doctor. So, Babuji—five weeks, give me time. Then I will start cleaning and meditation." There is no heart attack which prevents a man from meditating today. In fact, he should meditate today if possible, if he is to overcome this heart attack and step into one of two paths. You know the famous experiment involving the particles of matter—they always follow a particular path. You open two paths and, for no reason, some go through this, some go through that. Nobody is able to say why.

Perhaps they are also having hidden samskaras which guide them to this way or to that way!

If it is my destiny to die, I should die meditating. I remember a preceptor in our country in India who had a heart attack, and stopped meditation. Babuji was very upset. He said, "This man is so stupid. He is going to die. The best way of dying is to sit in meditation thinking of the Master when the door into eternity is opened automatically. Instead of that, he is not meditating, he is taking medicines and he is relying upon some fools, astrologers. What is this I am telling you?" These were Babuji's words.

(p.108-109)

— ❖ —

So, those of you who would not subject to extreme pain must understand that you cannot enjoy extreme pleasure, too—in no field of human existence. Then we are at the midpoint—as I repeat, gentle swings. No pleasure, no pain, no danger, no frustration, but a benign, calm, fulfilled existence. Then I begin to think of my Self. My problems in existence are over. I know now I have a Self inside. I seek someone who can tell me what it is. He says, "Sit and meditate. I cannot tell you what it is. You have to perceive it, experience it in yourself." Through this meditation I become aware that there is something in me which is not the **me** I thought I was. I begin to go more and more towards it. As I go more and more towards the east, I am inevitably going more and more away from the west. No need to renounce. By the fact of turning inwards, I am turning away from the external. Automatically, the renunciation that people have tried for centuries to achieve and failed, is in my hands, is in my grasp. I renounce without renouncing, because I am walking towards the right thing, the right goal—my inner Self. (p.133-134)

— ❖ —

Therefore, something which is very commonly misunderstood in Sahaj Marg—that we begin at the sixth step of yoga. Why? One, two, three, four, five—they don't bother us. Six, seven, and eight—they apply to us, because through *dhyana, dharana* becomes possible, *samadhi* becomes possible. The other five steps we are supposed to have already created for ourselves by right living **before** we come to the guru. *Asana* is only sitting in a right pose for the duration of the meditation. We are supposed to have created that ability, not lounge around like these pampered Americans, you know, and Europeans. They are not comfortable anywhere. Give them six cushions, they want a seventh. Give them seven, they want a ninth. Put them in an air-conditioned room, they must have the temperature exact, and you know, they are fiddling around with the thermostat. Put them in a soundproof room, yet the dog barking next door seems to penetrate to their ears, and they want the dog in the next house chained up and put away. How will they ever meditate? (p.137)

What is Sahaj Marg
A Preceptor's Guide, Volume I
Shri P. Rajagopalachari

Then we come to meditation. Meditation has been defined as thinking constantly about something. Rest, you all know why we meditate. But please remember that meditation is only a technique. It is not an end in itself. And this is exemplified by the often repeated fact that many people just go into meditation and start snoring and, you know, they are not aware of anything else, it is done in a mechanical way. And they enjoy the meditation rather than do the meditation. And Babuji used to say, "This is a mechanical thing and they have no progress at all." Because when we meditate, it has to be a dynamic process in which the goal is always in our view. That is, a movement towards the goal is involved. Otherwise it is like sitting in a static train. Even a TGV, you know, if it is drawn up in the yards of the Paris stations, and is destined to go only tomorrow morning, if I sit in it, it's not going to take me anywhere. It must move.

So meditation is a process, it is not an end in itself. I say this because I find often preceptors say, "Meditate and everything is solved." Nothing is solved by meditation. By meditation we meditate. What do we achieve by meditation?—then if people ask, you see—well, by mastering the ability to think continuously of something, I gain a regulatory control over my own mind. I have now the possibility of applying that mind where I choose. It is able to reveal to me the truth of whatever I seek. So at its peak, meditation can do nothing but serve as an instrument of revelation, because the mind is perfected, the mind is regulated, and the mind becomes one-pointed and now I can use it for everything except to know God. (p.52-53)

— ❖ —

So why faith in the Master? For this reason you see: that by meditation I clear this instrument of my perception, "The ultimate instrument," as Babuji said, "for your destruction, and for your elevation." (p.64)

— ❖ —

Therefore if we wish to change our destiny, as we call it, our future, build it afresh, renew it—we have to work with our thought, with the mind. Therefore raja yoga operates with the mind, through the mind. That is why we have to meditate. That is why meditation, though it is only regulation of the mind, is very necessary, very vital. Because the mind has to be under our regulatory control. Otherwise, it runs amok. Like an elephant that has gone *must,* as we say, and it is destructive. (p.124)

— ❖ —

...in fact all these things we are doing are to invite His grace. Sadhana alone can achieve nothing. As I told you, meditation is only something to clean your mind, regulate it, make it an instrument of revelation. What can you do with it for finding God? (p.229)

— ❖ —

Transmission, when you are light, gives you the feeling of going deep into the meditation. Transmission, when it is gross, produces vibrations, all these funny things, you see. The subtler it is, the more you must feel that there has been nothing happening in the meditation. (p.265)

A Preceptor's Guide, Volume II
Shri P. Rajagopalachari

We are telling ourselves that we are powerless. The cause is the over-activity or the hyperactivity of the mind which is indulging in so many fantasies, but not resting upon itself. And this is the secret of meditation: that we bring this hyperactive mind to rest, a state of total rest which becomes *samadhi*. And then you find the power of the Original Mind is now becoming manifest within itself, not to be used or misused, but just to be aware that it exists, and to be used by turning it upon yourself for your own ultimate spiritual release from this world. And for the further stages of spiritual evolution which we call realisation, *layavastha*, etc. (p.111-112)

— ❖ —

I think in Courmettes I had a discussion about meditation and cleaning, what is the basic difference. The basic difference is that in meditation your mind is brought to a state of passivity applied to a single object to promote or develop concentration, and there it rests. There is no question of will power during meditation. In cleaning there is no meditation, there is only the application of will power used to remove grossness, impurities, complexes... (p.125)

— ❖ —

Special Techniques of Meditation For Checking the Mind's Tendency Towards Indulgences and to Check Improprieties in Behaviour*

Babuji says: "To achieve correction of such gross tendencies, the point A of the heart region is used for meditation. It is highly effective in correcting self-indulging tendencies. It is very useful to check the distracting power of the opposite sex, especially in male abhyasis."

Now you all know where the point A is. It is written in *Efficacy of Raja Yoga*. Starting from the left nipple, you measure two fingers width, locate a point, and then below that, three fingers width is A and then another two fingers width down is point B. Locate it in yourself by measuring it with your own fingers, and then meditate on that point.

"a) Meditation on point 'A': The abhyasi should be instructed to fix his attention on the point A with the thought that all the men and women of the world are his brothers and sisters."

This is a very positive meditation. We don't say, "Oh, such-and-such person is not my sister," because then she is something else. Especially for males, you see. You must have the positive thought, meditating on this point, all in this world are my brothers and sisters. And please don't make... (bringing the exclusion principle) and say, "except..."[laughter] [he laughs] Yes, there is always a temptation to exclude something, you see, which for the moment is exciting. This is a total principle you know, that all are my brothers and sisters.

* This passage and the two following ones have been published with the permission of Shri P. Rajagopalachari, who advised abhyasis to discuss them with their preceptor.

The one that my Master or my destiny chooses to be my wife will eventually be my wife. If she is already my wife, she is already my wife. If she is already my mother or sister, she is already there. This is the blood relationship. But in the spiritual principle **all** are my brothers and sisters. Because Babuji told me once when my son got into the system, he said, "You must treat him as a spiritual brother, not a spiritual son." And once I introduced my brother's son who is probably forty years my junior in age to Sahaj Marg, and immediately after the sitting he got up and hugged me and said "Hello, brother." [he laughs] [laughter] For him it was a liberation of sorts, you see, that an uncle has now become a brother.

So this is to be done with a mind which longs for correction. I know there are many people who are perverted, and who don't wish to change their pervert tendencies or their wrong deeds. Of such people you can expect nothing. And for them this technique will not work, because in the beginning they will refuse to employ it. They will say, "Why? I am happy as I am." This is for the sincere seeker, who, being aware of the tendencies of his mind, and who, deploring his own activities in the field of action, wishes to correct himself sincerely, honestly, towards correcting himself and divinising himself eventually. For such a person this technique is most effective.

"Meditate on point A, with the thought that all the men and women of the world are his brothers and sisters. This meditation is to be done just before going to bed," (That is, instead of the cleaning process which you do. If you don't do it at the time it is stipulated, you normally do it at night, before the prayer-meditation. This should be just before the prayer-meditation.) "for not more than ten minutes."

Now people may ask why. Because if this feeling becomes too deeply implanted in the heart, you know, instead of just producing a clean attitude towards humanity, it may produce what we deplore in Sahaj Marg, a running away from life all together. You know, that all are brothers and sisters, how can I ever marry this girl? So you feel the need to give up life, give up marriage, become celibate, on the way to the jungle. It goes to the opposite extreme. Everything has an optimum time, an optimum effect, and for this meditation the optimum is ten minutes.

"My Master has said that generally women do not require this meditation, as they are comparatively free from the restless tendencies." [he laughs] [laughter] Since my Master has said it I won't question it. [laughter] "But if a sister abhyasi is a victim of such tendencies, then she may be advised to follow the process with a slight modification in the process. She should think that all divine gifts are available to her, and that all men and women of the world think they are brothers and sisters and that her thought is one with theirs."

It's a rather convoluted way of achieving the same thing. She doesn't think that all men and women are her sisters. She thinks divine blessings are coming to her. That all the men and women of the world are meditating on this thought that they are all brothers and sisters, and that she is part of that thought. I think this is necessary in the case of women, because, as you know, they are the propagators of the race. Through women, of course, humanity breeds, you see, and if this tendency that all are brothers and sisters, and the tendency to celibacy and all these things go too far, and too many people, I mean, nowadays it may be desirable that the population is limited but in the future it might not be so desirable. So women are to practise the same technique on A point meditation with this slight change. You will receive it in writing so you can study it later.

Then:

"b) Meditation on Point 'B': Fix the attention on the point B and imagine that all your impurities and grossnesses are going out from point B from the front of the body."

In the general cleaning which you do, it is all from the back of the body as smoke or vapour. In this case it is to imagine that they are going out from the front especially from the point B.

"Imagine that as this process is going on the glow of the Atman, the soul, begins to appear from behind."

It is like cleaning a dirty light and as the cleaning goes on, the light is coming out more and more bright. So here also as this cleaning on point B goes on you have to imagine that the dirt and the filth all accumulated there is coming out. And as this cleaning is proceeding a glow begins to appear from behind which is the light of the Atman, you see, the soul. "This process is to be done in the morning, before beginning morning meditation but never more than for ten minutes."

So in the case of both these techniques, meditation on point A and B, the time is limited to ten minutes. Both are available for men and women—point A with a certain change in the technique for women only, but otherwise there is no difference.

"These two meditations on points A and B are very useful in correcting the disturbed tendencies of the mind. Since this tendency exists in the majority of cases these meditations can be safely advised to almost all abhyasis without exception."

(p.127-131)

— ❖ —

...Babuji has said that, "For women there are no specific times for meditation. They can sit when they choose." Even when they cook. Babuji has said, "If they cook in the thought they are cooking for the Divine, under the orders of the Divine, and that the Divine is going to eat it, it is sufficient for them." You see the spiritual tradition, it is enormously generous where women are concerned, very flexible, very understanding of the compulsions under which women exist, not only today but from eons past. (p.158)

— ❖ —

..."Women should not be allowed to meditate upon the form of the teacher or preceptor. The preceptor should be careful that no personal attachment is allowed to develop in her for the preceptor. For this purpose" (here is a way of doing it), "for this purpose, women can meditate [he laughs] on the form of their husbands." [laughter]

But, it is not written here, you won't find it in the written copy, but Master always said, "Only if he is deserving." The same principle, you see, that the form upon which we meditate should deserve that attention from us.

"A better course for women should be to meditate at the point of the heart, here, thinking that she is meditating on Him, who is all-pervading," (You see, therefore there is a way of meditating upon the Master, but instead of adopting the form, think of him as the 'all-pervading' and meditate) "and who is pervading in her husband too."

So, here you bring in the, you know, the union of the all-pervading and the husband as one possible entity, you see, so that the husband is not divorced in your thought from the Master. You are able to think of both simultaneously. Meditating on Him who is all-pervading and pervading in the husband too. It is a fact that the Almighty is pervading in the husband too, whatever he may be today.

"...and who is pervading in her husband too, this will strengthen the *pativrata dharma* of the woman, the *dharma* of leading a chaste life."

Incidentally it will also benefit the husband because he is part of her meditation. So I think, you know, in denying the meditation on the form of the Master to the women, Master is only giving in its place a better technique for the women. (p.159)

— ❖ —

I think this tendency we have to overcome and accept with our hearts that what happens during meditation, as my Master said, "Anything that happens in meditation is good." Even if it is the worst possible thing according to our minds. Because it is only showing a release of what is hidden inside, locked up inside, buried inside. And when it comes out it is going to give us some problem. But it is a problem only when you treat it as a problem. If you think of it as something going out, and in the very going out, giving you some relief, then it becomes very easy. (p.193)

— ❖ —

Meditation ... It is like putting a seed in the ground and doing something to it, you know, pushing it from above, deeper and deeper and deeper, as deep as it will go. In the heart there is no limit. It is not the ground that there can be a limit to it. The heart is, perhaps, the ultimate abyss, something which is bottomless. That is why there is so much going in it that we do not know of, so much going on in it that we would like and not like perhaps too, so much more that can be put into it. (p.219)

— ❖ —

It is, I think, a rather egotistical idea that we do anything. If spirituality teaches us anything and if we are to learn anything, it is this ultimate lesson that we are but observers. This is what meditation is designed to inculcate in us, into us, progressively. And the whole idea of observing and reporting, diary maintaining is merely for this, precisely for this purpose—that we learn to separate the observer from the field of observation which is also myself. The higher self to be separated from the lower activity of the samskara-led life. ...

When we start meditating, and if you are serious about it, and if you go about it properly, you must achieve this separation of the real self, the inner self, from this mundane self, which is but a machine run through the five senses under the control of the mind with an intellect supposed to guide it. (p.245-246)

— ❖ —

We are still concerned, obsessed, with our petty human miserable existence; meditating, with the mind on the boyfriend or girlfriend; meditating, thinking the house is going to set on fire when we are not there; meditating, wondering who is going to look after the cats and dogs that we have unnecessarily adopted. Whose fault is this? (p.263)

A Preceptor's Guide, Volume III
Shri P. Rajagopalachari

So when we have come to this *karma* and *gyana* aspect, done our practice faithfully, systematically, intelligently, regularly, using such knowledge as we have got, but which is being sharpened all the time because in meditation the mind is making itself one-pointed, progressively, with greater and greater directness and efficiency, we are able to achieve a state of perfect work, perfect understanding—nothing more. (p.159)

— ❖ —

So the idea is that there must be a certain degree of freedom from the body and its needs before you can really sit down and meditate. This is the fundamental principle. Not everybody can sit on a bed of nails and meditate. Not everybody can sit on cold stone floors in the winter in Shahjahanpur and meditate. Not everybody can meditate on an empty stomach. Therefore, the minimum necessary to liberate your mind from the troubles and the travails of the body inflicting themselves into the presence of the mind are to be avoided, so that we can go about the business of meditation. This is the fundamental principle underlying our providing such comfort as we are able to provide, and which we want to provide. It is nothing more than that. (p.203-204)

At night you see the branches waving outside your window, and you think somebody is waving at you to welcome you outside. Our senses are more easily accepting illusions than reality. Our whole life, in that sense, is illusory. We have not been trained to see reality yet. Therefore, in the ancient wisdom, we close our eyes, we suspend all activity, sit at peace and turn inwards to that ultimate organ which never tells a lie—the heart.

In yoga, very literally, we refuse to see with the eyes; we block our ears, because when we are meditating on the heart, and we are absorbed, we don't hear anything; taste doesn't function anymore, touch doesn't function anymore. All the five senses are sort of synthesized into one grand sense and pushed into the heart, from which we see, we hear, we smell, we taste, we touch, everything. (p.205)

Down Memory Lane, Volume I
Shri P. Rajagopalachari

A few days later, we had gone to Shri Vira Raghavan's place for Sunday satsangh. Master was staying with us at *Gayathri*. As soon as we returned home, Master asked me, "Are you free for a few moments?" I said I of course had all the time in the world for him. He took me upstairs to the room which we rather pretentiously called our library, from which my Master did all the important spiritual work that he did when he was with us. There he said, "Today by the grace of Lalaji Maharaj your mother has been granted her liberation. It was done during the satsangh. Now I shall give you the proof of it. Please sit in meditation." I protested that I needed no proof, but he insisted. Rather unusually, he did not sit in his usual seat, but put on his cap—which he does only when Lalaji Sahib pays a visit—and sat next to me, facing the empty seat in front of us—the seat of the Master! He said, "Now your mother will transmit to you. Please meditate." I sat in meditation. I immediately felt as if my mother had taken me on her lap, and was lovingly caressing me, crooning to me. I had tears in my eyes. Master terminated the sitting after some ten minutes, and asked me what I had felt. I related the experience to him. He said, "Yes! That was exactly what happened. Now see, that is the mother's love which you experienced. But now she wants to go. Who will stay in this unfortunate and ill-destined world after liberation! She is in a hurry to go. She is blessing the Mission, and blessing it to grow and grow!" (p.15)

— ❖ —

The next morning, the 14th of April, I had a wonderful experience. I was sitting in a chair next to my father's body, and suddenly felt transmission coming to me from a point just above my father's chest. I closed my eyes and went into meditation. I could clearly see my father transmitting to me. It was a very tender, love-filled transmission, and lasted about fifteen minutes. Then suddenly the source shifted to a position a few inches to the left, and I saw my Master, Babuji Maharaj, seated there transmitting to me. It was as if Babuji Maharaj had come to show me that Appa was with him, and that there was really nothing called death, and to reassure me that all was well with my father. (p.176)

— ❖ —

I have been an ardent admirer of Vivekananda, and have read his works again and again since my college days in Calcutta, going to his books repeatedly for guidance as well as for inspiration over a period spanning very nearly five decades. I was drawn to that great figure ever since I visited the Belur Math in Calcutta for the first time, way back in the forties. I was influenced by his example to such an extent that I commenced the practice of *asanas* and *pranayama* without any guidance, on my own, and sort of graduated into meditation, also without any formal guidance. There have been many occasions when reading his books has moved me to tears.

I got into the habit of going to visit the Ramakrishna Math and there to sit in silent meditation amidst the clamour and din of their own ritualistic worship at the shrine of Shri Ramakrishna. Such visits to the Ramakrishna Math became something of a habit with me whenever I was troubled in my mind and needed the solace of deep meditation. It is something of a pity that the lay disciples were made to perform the traditional *puja* at the Paramahamsa's shrine, instead of being instructed to sit in silent meditation. I have found this system of ritualistic *puja* prevalent even in the Ramakrishna Maths outside India which I have visited. I understand that the *sannyasis* do meditation, but I have never been able to understand why the lay devotees are not permitted to meditate. This sort of discrimination is there, unfortunately, in most of such organizations which I have come across. (p.298-299)

Glossary

AAKAAR: Form.

ABHYAS: Practice.

ABHYASI: Aspirant, one who practises yoga in order to achieve union with God.

ACHARAS: Religious observance.

ADI GURU: Original Guru; Lalaji, in Sahaj Marg.

AGYA CHAKRA : See Ajna Chakra.

AHAM BRAHMASMI : I am Brahma.

AJAPA: Meditation without utterance of any mantra.

AJNA CHAKRA (or AGYA CHAKRA): The fire point located between the eyebrows. *Trikuti.*

ANANT-KI-OR: *Towards Infinity.*

ANTARYAMI: The God within; the In-Dweller.

ANUBHAV: Intuitional perception or personal experience in the realm of Nature or God.

ASAN (or ASANA): Posture. Also the third limb of Patanjali's Ashtanga Yoga.

ASHRAM: Ashram comes from the Sanskrit *shreyas* which applies, in the spiritual sense, to the growth of benefits which are connected to the higher level. An ashram is also a kind of refuge, a place of retreat from today's life. Ashrams in Sahaj Marg are dedicated to meditation only, all other activities are normally not allowed in the Ashram. An Ashram is usually charged by the Master, who creates a special atmosphere of spirituality in which we meditate.

ASHTANG YOGA (ASHTANGA YOGA): Patanjali described yoga as having eight limbs: *yama, niyama, asana, pranayama, pratyahara, dharana, dhyana* and *samadhi*.

ATMAN: Soul

BASANT (or BASANT PANCHAMI): Fifth day of spring in the lunar calendar. It is also Lalaji's birthday.

BELUR MATH: Ramakrishna Math at Belur, near Calcutta,Bengal.

BENGAL: An eastern state of India.

BEWAKOOF: Fool.

BHAGAVAD GITA: See Gita.

BHAJAN: Chanted prayer.

BHAKTI: Devotion.

BHAKTAS: Devotees.

BHANG: A type of intoxicating drug used in India.

BHAVA: Expression of an inner condition; attitude of the mind.

BHOG (or BHOGA): Process of undergoing effects of impressions; experience; enjoyment.

BHRUVORMADHYE: Between the eyebrows.

BODH: Wisdom.

BODHI TREE: Tree under which Buddha is believed to have meditated to achieve nirvana.

BRAHM (or BRAHMAN): Centre; God; Ultimate.

BRAHMA: Lord of Creation.

BRAHMAASTRA: Weapons of Gods.

BRAHMAND MANDAL: Mental sphere, supra-material sphere, cosmic region; sphere where everything manifests under a subtle shape before taking place in the material world.

CHARAS: A type of intoxicating drug used in India.

CHAKRA: Centre of super-vital forces located in different parts of the body; figuratively called lotus.

CHINMAYANANDA: An Indian guru of the twentieth century.

CLEANING: 1. Specific meditation done at the end of each day by all Sahaj Marg abhyasis. 2. Use of will power by the Master or preceptors in utilizing *pranahuti* to remove subtle distortions, coverings and impurities that impede an abhyasi's development.

COURMETTES: A small resort in southern France.

DAKSHINESHWAR: A place near Calcutta, India.

DARSHAN: Vision of someone's inner reality.

DHARANA: Mental focus; concentration (sixth limb of Patanjali's Ashtanga Yoga).

DHARMA: A term with many applications, depending on the context: duty, righteousness; destined way; truth; virtue; that which upholds.

DHYAN (or DHYANA): Meditation (seventh limb of Patanjali's Ashtanga Yoga).

GANJA: A type of intoxicating drug used in India.

GAYATRI (or GAYATHRI) JAPA: Repeated chanting of the gayatri mantra.

GAYATHRI: Shri P. Rajagopalachari's home in Madras, named after the gayathri mantra.

GITA (BHAGAWAT GITA or BHAGAVAD GITA): Divine knowledge given to Arjuna by Lord Krishna in the Mahabharata. Also, the Bhagavad Gita, or "Song of God," an essential scripture of Hinduism, containing a portion of the epic, Mahabharata.

GRANTHI: Knot.

GUNAS: The three qualities of nature in Hindu philosophy: *sattva, rajas* and *tamas*.

GURU GOVIND SINGH: The ninth Guru of the Sikhs.

GURU PASHU: People who become devoted to the Master's physical form.

GYAN (or GYANA): Supreme wisdom or knowledge leading to Realisation.

HASHISH: A type of intoxicating drug used in India.

HATHA YOGA: The first four steps of Patanjali's Ashtanga Yoga. The practice of yoga concerning the physical body.

HAQ: Right.

INDRIYAS: Ten senses/organs of Indian philosophy, subdivided as *gyana* and *karma* indriyas. The former are five senses pertaining to perception, knowledge or wisdom, while the latter are five senses pertaining mainly to action.

ISHTA DEVATAS: Chosen deity.

ISHWARIYA PRAKASH: Divine Light.

JANMA: Birth.

JAPA: Repetition of a mantra.

JURASSIC PARK: Spielberg's movie about dinosaurs.

KABIR (or KABIRDAS): A fifteenth century Indian saint and spiritual poet.

KALA MATA: An Indian goddess, worshipped mainly in Bengal.

KARMA: Action.

KRISHNA (or LORD KRISHNA): Most recent incarnation of Vishnu.

KRIYA: Action

LAKSHYA: Goal

LAYAWASTHA (or LAYAVASTHA): The state of mergence.

MAHARAJ: Literally supreme king, used as a title for a great person.

MAHATMA: Great soul, saint.

MAHESH: An Indian god; god of destruction.

MANAPAKKAM: Name of the place in Madras where the Babuji Memorial Ashram is built.

MAHAPARANIRVANA: The great transcendental nirvana or emancipation.

MANTRA (or MANTHRA): A sacred phrase or word, usually for repetitious chanting.

MANU: Name of a great saint who framed the codes of conduct.

MAYA: Phenomenal appearance. It is really a power of God. All manifestation or expansion which seems illusory is the play or maya. Illusion.

MEHER BABA: An Indian saint of the twentieth century.

MOORTHY (or MOORTI): Idol; sculpture of a deity.

NANAK: Adi Guru of the Sikhs.

NASIKAGRE: The tip of the nose.

NETI-NETI: The principle of 'not this, not this'.

NIRVIKALPA SAMADHI: Samadhi in which we are not conscious; ecstasy with the loss of the world-consciousness; consciousness of abstract.

NISHKAMA KARMA: Desireless action.

NIYAMA: Subjected laws which must be followed. They are purity, contentment, austerity, self-study, self-abandonment (devotion to God). The second limb of Patanjali's Ashtanga Yoga.

OM: The sacred syllable 'Aum'.

PANDIT RAMESHWAR PRASAD: Babuji's Gurubhai, co-disciple of Babuji.

PARAMATMAN: The supreme soul.

PARATATVA: Transcendental concept or the 'Supreme'.

PARDA: veil.

PATANJALI: Ancient Indian scholar who wrote the Yoga Sutras.

PATIVRATA DHARMA: The way of family life to be followed by a chaste wife in which the husband is supreme.

PINDA PRADESH: Material sphere; the heart region.

PRALAYA: State of dissolution, applied not to the whole universe but only to a part of it.

PRANA: Life, breath.

PRANAHUTI: Process of yogic transmission; derived from *prana* meaning life and *ahuti* meaning offering. Offering of life force by the guru into the disciple's heart.

PRANA VAYU: Life giving air or oxygen.

PRANAYAMA: The fourth limb of Patanjali's Ashtanga Yoga. Breathing exercises. Derived from *prana* (life, breath) and *ayama* (to restrain). The regulation of prana.

PRASAD: Divinised food, usually sweet. Food that is partaken and thus charged by the divine.

PRATYAHARA: The inner withdrawal of the mind. The fifth step of Patanjali's Yoga Sutra.

PRAVACHAN: Divine discourse.

PRECEPTOR: An abhyasi prepared and permitted by the Master to impart spiritual training through the utilization of *pranahuti* or yogic transmission.

PUJA: A physical ritualistic act of worshipping a deity (in Sahaj Marg, the meditation practice).

PUJARI: Literally, one who does *puja*; equivalent of the priest in a Hindu Temple.

RAJA YOGA (or RAJ YOGA): Ancient system or science followed by the great rishis and saints which helped them to realise the Self or God. Usually used for meditative practices, as distinguished from hatha yoga.

RAMAKRISHNA MATH: An ashram of the Ramakrishna Mission. (N)

RAMAKRISHNA PARAMAHAMSA: Saint who lived in Dakshineshwar during the nineteenth century and who was Swami Vivekananda's Master, on whose name Ramakrishna Mission is established.

RAMANUJA: One of the three acharyas; founder of the Vishisht-advaita system of Vedanta philosophy.

RAMAYANA: One of the epic stories in India: the life of Rama, an incarnation of Vishnu.

RISHI: Saint; seer; one who has realised Self (usually through meditative practices).

SADHAK: Disciple who practises a sadhana.

SADHANA: Spiritual practice.

SAHAJ MARG: Natural path, simple path.

SAHAJ SAMADHI: Natural *samadhi*, considered the highest samadhi: simultaneity of total external awareness with total inner emptiness or absorption.

SAHASRA: Thousand.

SAHASRA-DAL-KAMAL: Lotus of a thousand petals. Chakra at the top of the head.

SAHAVAS: Living together.

SAHEB (or SAHIB): Hindi equivalent of Sir; a respectful form of address to a man.

SALWAR KAMIJ: An Indian dress for the ladies consisting of loose pants and a long overblouse.

SAMADHI: The eighth and final step of Patanjali's Ashtanga Yoga; original balance. State in which we stay attached to Reality. In Sahaj Marg, the return to the original condition, which reigned in the beginning. Babuji split the word into *sama*, meaning balance, and *adhi*, meaning original or ancient.

SAMSKARAS (or SANSKARAS): Impressions. In Sahaj Marg, considered to be obstacles for spiritual progress.

SANDHYA: Meeting point between day and night.

SANKALPA: A subtle idea; an act of will.

SANKARACHARYA: Ancient saint of India, who propounded *advaita* (non-dualism) philosophy.

SANNYASI (or SANYASI): One who has renounced the worldly responsibilities and leads a solitary life of celibacy and asceticism.

SANSKRIT: Culture; also name of the ancient language of India.

SANSTHA: Spiritual tradition; organization; group.

SAPTA-RISHIS: Seven rishis.

SANGHA: Togetherness.

SAPTALOK: All the seven worlds.

SAT: Truth; Reality.

SATSANGH (or SATSANG): 1. Spiritual assembly; 2. Being with Reality.

SATYA SAI BABA: An Indian guru of the twentieth century.

SHAKTI: Power.

SHANKARACHARYAS: A title much like the pope, given to the head of a spiritual organization in India. Coming in the tradition of the first Sankaracharya.

SHANTI: Peace.

SHAT: Six.

SIDDHIS: Capacity or power to perform miracles, usually achieved through meditative practices.

SITTING: A session of meditation, usually lasting from thirty minutes to an hour, in which the Master or a preceptor meditates with a group or an individual for the purpose of cleaning and transmission.

SOOKSHMA SHARIR: Astral body, subtle body.

STHIRAM SUKHAM ASANAM: Steady, comfortable posture.

STHOOLA RUPA: Gross form.

SURAT: A town in Gujarat.

SUTRA: Literally 'thread'; here an 'aphorism'.

SWAMIJI: A title given to spiritual leaders in several spiritual organizations in India.

TAI CHI: A Chinese spiritual practice.

TAMASHA: Drama; play.

TANTRIC TRADITION: Tantra shastra.

TAPAS: Literally means heat, and indicates the heat generated by the friction of intense spiritual practice.

TAPASVI: One who does *tapasya.*

TAPASYA: Ardent, single-minded, focused ascetic practices to purify the soul and attract Divine grace.

TATHASTU: Let it be so.

THIK HAI: It's okay.

TOTAPURI: The preceptor of Ramakrishna Paramahamsa.

TOURNESOLS: French word for sunflower.

TRISHUL: A three-pronged weapon of Shiva; trident.

TRIKUTI: The point above the nose between the two eyebrows; one of the points of concentration.

UNPAD: Illiterate.

UPANISHADS: Vedantic part of the Vedas (Jnana Kanda).

VALMIKI: An ancient saint of India, the author of the epic Ramayana.

VASHISHTA: An ancient rishi of India, preceptor of Lord Rama.

VISHA PARIKSHA: The acid test.

VISHNU: One of the Hindu trinity, God as preserver.

VISHWAMITRA: An ancient rishi of India.

VIVEKANANDA: A great saint of India who lived in the early twentieth century and was a disciple of Ramakrishna.

YAGNAVALKYA: A great ancient Indian rishi.

YAMA: The first step of Patanjali's Ashtanga Yoga. Refers to the purity of body and mind. Also, Lord of Death.

YOGA: Literally meaning the unity of the soul with the supreme soul. Also acceptable to mean practices that lead to the state of oneness.

YOGA DARSHAN: The work of Patanjali.

YOGI: One who practises yoga; one who achieves union with the Absolute.

References

SHRI RAM CHANDRA OF FATEHGARH, U.P.

Truth Eternal, 3rd ed., Shri Ram Chandra Mission, Shahjahanpur, India, 1987.

SHRI RAM CHANDRA OF SHAHJAHANPUR, U.P.

The Autobiography of Ram Chandra, vol. I, 2nd ed., Shri Ram Chandra Mission, Shahjahanpur, India, 1980.

————, vol. II, Shri Ram Chandra Mission, Shahjahanpur, India, 1976.

Complete Works of Ram Chandra, vol. I, Shri Ram Chandra Mission, North American Publishing Committee, Pacific Grove, CA, USA, 1989.

————, vol. II, Shri Ram Chandra Mission, North American Publishing Committee, Pacific Grove, CA, USA, 1991.

Letters of the Master, vol. I, ed. by Thomas J. Whitlam, Shri Ram Chandra Mission, North American Publishing Committee, Pacific Grove, CA, USA, 1992.

————, vol. II, ed. by Thomas J. Whitlam, Shri Ram Chandra Mission, North American Publishing Committee, Pacific Grove, CA, USA, 1992.

Messages Universal, Shri Ram Chandra Mission, Shahjahanpur, India, 1983.

SHRI PARTHASARATHI RAJAGOPALACHARI

Blossoms in the East, Shri Ram Chandra Mission, Shahjahanpur, India, 1977.

Down Memory Lane, vol. I, Shri Ram Chandra Mission, North American Publishing Committee, Pacific Grove, CA, USA, 1993.

The Fruit of the Tree, Shri Ram Chandra Mission, Shahjahanpur, India, 1988.

The Garden of Hearts, Shri Ram Chandra Mission, Shahjahanpur, India, 1980.

Heart of the Lion, Shri Ram Chandra Mission, North American Publishing Committee, Pacific Grove, CA, USA, 1993.

Heart to Heart, vol. I, Shri Ram Chandra Mission, Shahjahanpur, India, 1988.

————, vol. II, Shri Ram Chandra Mission, North American Publishing Committee, Pacific Grove, CA, USA, 1991.

————, vol. III, Shri Ram Chandra Mission, North American Publishing Committee, Pacific Grove, CA, USA, 1994.

India in the West, Shri Ram Chandra Mission, Shahjahanpur, India, 1973.

In His Footsteps, vol. I, Shri Ram Chandra Mission, North American Publishing Committee, Pacific Grove, CA, USA, 1988.

————, vol. II, Shri Ram Chandra Mission, North American Publishing Committee, Pacific Grove, CA, USA, 1993. (No significant quotations on meditation have been selected.)

Love and Death, Shri Ram Chandra Mission, North American Publishing Committee, Pacific Grove, CA, USA, 1992.

My Master, 6th ed., Shri Ram Chandra Mission, Shahjahanpur, India, 1989.

A Preceptor's Guide, vol. II, Shri Ram Chandra Mission, North American Publishing Committee, Pacific Grove, CA, USA, 1990.

————, vol. III, Shri Ram Chandra Mission, North American Publishing Committee, Pacific Grove, CA, USA, 1990.

The Principles of Sahaj Marg, vol. I, Shri Ram Chandra Mission, Shahjahanpur, India, 1986.

————, vol. II, Shri Ram Chandra Mission, Shahjahanpur, India, 1987.

————, vol. III, Shri Ram Chandra Mission, Shahjahanpur, India, 1987.

————, vol. IV, Shri Ram Chandra Mission, Shahjahanpur, India, 1988.

————, vol. V, Shri Ram Chandra Mission, Shahjahanpur, India, 1989.

————, vol. VI, Shri Ram Chandra Mission, Shahjahanpur, India, 1990.

———, vol.VII, Shri Ram Chandra Mission, Shahjahanpur, India, 1993.

———, vol.VIII, Shri Ram Chandra Mission, Shahjahanpur, India, 1994.

Proceedings of the Preceptor's Seminar, Shri Ram Chandra Mission, Shahjahanpur, India, 1992. (No significant quotations on meditation have been selected.)

Proceedings of the Seminar on Sahaj Marg (Vorauf—Munich, Germany), Shri Ram Chandra Mission, Germany, 1985.

Religion and Spirituality, Shri Ram Chandra Mission, North American Publishing Committee, Pacific Grove, CA, USA, 1992.

Revealing the Personality, Shri Ram Chandra Mission, Denmark, 1992.

Role of the Master in Human Evolution, Shri Ram Chandra Mission, Munich, West Germany, 1986.

Sahaj Marg in Europe, Shri Ram Chandra Mission, Shahjahanpur, India, 1976.

What Is Sahaj Marg?—A Preceptor's Guide, vol. I, Shri Ram Chandra Mission, North American Publishing Committee, Pacific Grove, CA, USA, 1988.

This is only a partial listing of Sahaj Marg publications. For a complete listing, please write to:

Shri Ram Chandra Mission
Post Office Box 269
Molena, GA 30258 USA